LIFE

The Biggest Game of All

One Life to Live, so Many Choices

Gabe:
    Helping other people
is truly a gift that
you have. Hope you
enjoy the book.

DAVID M. HOOF

David M. Hoof

11-6-22

ISBN 978-1-64140-006-0 (paperback)
ISBN 978-1-64140-516-4 (hardcover)
ISBN 978-1-64140-007-7 (digital)

Christian Faith Publishing, Inc.
832 Park Avenue
Meadville, PA 16335
www.christianfaithpublishing.com

Cover Art by David M. Hoof

Printed in the United States of America

DEDICATION

> *"So whether you eat or drink or whatever*
> *you do, do it all for the glory of God."*
> **—1 Corinthians 10:31**

This book is dedicated to the glory of God as this Bible verse was my inspiration to complete this book. Jesus offers the gift of Salvation to everyone, and I have given Him my heart and life. I now know what a profound effect God can have in one's life, and I want to share my life's story with as many as possible. God loves us all.

CONTENTS

Section II
America's Decisions
In This Changing World

Section III
Decisions Others Have Made
Assorted Stories

FOREWORD

Life can be wonderful, and life can be really bad.
There is a saying:
"Life is what you make it.
Always has been, always will be."
So simple, yet so true.

This book is about the game of life—that is, the game of my life and how my experiences, knowledge, and wisdom could benefit **YOUR** life. There are many choices to make. Some are small everyday choices, and some will result in lifelong changes. Some choices produce good life changes, and some choices produce not-so-good life changes. **Everybody is a player in the game of life**.

Some authors will write a book that says "I am successful, so just follow my direction and you will also be successful." This book is different as it is saying "Learn from my experiences." All people learn from their experiences, but it is the wise person who learns from someone else's experiences.

As I write this, I am seventy-one years old. That is seventy-one years of living. I have made a lot of decisions, some good choices, and some poor choices.

It is said we learn more from our mistakes than from our successes. Therefore, I have a lot to share that could help young adults avoid some of the pitfalls I have made and benefit by having a better, more rewarding life.

Learn from my experiences, and have a better life. **It is the lessons we learn from the past that show us the right path to the future.**

CHAPTER 1

Your Personal Game Coach

When you go out for a sport in high school or in college you will have a coach. If you want to be on the team you must agree to certain criteria. This is just an example:

1. You must be on time.
2. You must attend all practices.
3. You must be in the designated uniform.
4. You must participate in all conditioning exercises.
5. You must play in your assigned position on the team.
6. You must have a positive attitude.
7. You must follow all instructions by the coach.

You are surrendering your rights to make your own choices. Why would you do this??? You know that the coach has more experience than you or any of your friends on the team. Your goal is to win as a team. Therefore, you agree to surrender yourself and take direction from your coach. What about the Game of YOUR Life?

When playing any sport, it is important to have a good coach. The game of life is the same way. The best life coach is the one who loves you the most, and that is God. Many teens feel it is not "cool" or "acceptable" to be a believer in God, to ask Jesus to be their personal Savior, and let God show them the way. They do not want to surrender their lives to God, so they try to be independent and make their own decisions after talking to their friends. Some learn too late that this is not the wisest path. It is better to learn from a **life coach** to make good choices that produce good results.

Some decisions you will learn from, and some decisions change the direction of your life. We make some choices, and some choices make us.

In the foreword of this book, it is stated we learn more from our mistakes than from our successes. The reason is very easy to understand. When decisions yield the result we expect, we just go on with our lives, pat ourselves on the back, and say we did a good job. We normally do not spend a lot of time reflecting on our success, but when we make a bad decision where the results are not what we expected, we give great thought to what we can do to avoid the same situation from occurring again in our life. A lot of people will blame their bad decisions on someone else. One should be objective in reviewing their decisions. That is easier said than done. It has become part of our culture to blame others for bad things that happen to us when it is really our actions or lack of actions that caused the situation to occur.

A lot of people think success is getting ahead of another person. More money, bigger cars, bigger houses, bigger vacations—these are examples of how most people look at success. Have you heard the expression "the one with the most toys wins"? Just remember, there is another saying: **"You can't take it with you."**

I think **real success is simply getting ahead of yourself.** If your life is constantly improving, you are successful. Improving has a different meaning to different people. To some, it is the newest Apple iPhone, and to others, it is a hot meal. To others still, it is getting closer to God, learning about His Word in the Bible, and doing His work. I have learned it is the third direction that yields the most self-improvement and success. Remember, **"you don't know what you don't know."** There is so much to learn about life and what really brings true happiness. The Bible is full of great advice on how you can learn to live your life better.

11

As one travels the journey of life, they will hit a number of **dangerous** situations. If you know what these are, you can avoid them and provide for a better, safer, and more rewarding life. I ran into a number of these in my life, and I have learned a lot I would have done differently. Many people think they don't get a second chance at life and only have one chance at the game of life. However, when God offers Salvation to anyone who asks Him, they get a second chance at life. This is a new life where God is your **Life Coach** and much more.

It is my desire to help the young people of today have the knowledge to make better decisions than I did. As you journey through life, you will find your attitude determines your destiny.

Henry Ford (1863–1947), the founder of the Ford Motor Company, stated,

**"Whether you think you can,
or you think you can't—
you're right."**

It was very late in life when I asked Jesus to be my Lord and personal Savior. I asked Him to forgive my sins and lead me to the type of life He has for me. In our lives, we will have **missed opportunities**. One of my missed opportunities was I waited until I was sixty-eight years old to make the decision to ask Jesus to be my Lord and Savior and forgive my sins and allow God to lead the life He has planned for me.

God has a plan for each of us, and we need to listen to God and the Holy Spirit and take His direction.

God might not give you what you want, but He will always give you what you need.

Ask God to bless your life. You have so much to gain.

It is sad that 88 percent of children raised in evangelical homes leave the church at the age of eighteen, never to return (note 1-1).

It is also sad that 90 percent of children in homes where the father is not the spiritual leader will never find the Lord. I was not the spiritual leader in my home when our children were growing up, and I now understand that was a very big mistake. It was truly a missed opportunity to help my children grow up knowing God and His Word in the Bible.

The main purpose of writing this book is to increase young adults' desire to learn about God and His wonderful grace and mercy and avoid the mistakes I made during my life.

In life, most of us don't get a second chance to live a new life, so I challenge you to make the most of your life by taking some advice. When we ask God to bless our life, ask for His mercy and grace, and take the wonderful gift of Salvation through Jesus Christ, it truly is being "born again." Even though it's the same life in the flesh, it is a new spiritual life and a new beginning.

> *"Jesus replied, 'Very truly I tell you, no one can see the kingdom of God unless they are born again'"* (John 3:3).

Some will stop reading here, and that will be their **missed opportunity**.

CHAPTER 2

Your Game Plan

With the Game of Life, Everyday is a Game Day

I am a very fortunate person in so many ways. God has blessed my life even though I did not know it until later, when I was sixty-eight.

I have two wonderful daughters. When I lived in Knoxville, Tennessee, one day, my younger daughter was invited to attend a luncheon with her parents, at the University of Tennessee for honor students from the area high schools. The key speaker for the day was the UT quarterback, Peyton Manning. His presentation was about the choices we all make each day and our lifetime choices.

Peyton Manning stated it in very obvious and simple terms. He said we make decisions each day—like getting up in the morning and going to school. We also make life-changing decisions. These are the big decisions that direct the path of our lives.

At the time Peyton Manning was talking to the group of students, he had one more year before graduating and leaving to play professional football. Everyone was speculating whether he would skip his senior year and go professional or play football at UT for one more year. If he was injured during his senior year, it could affect or eliminate his professional career. What would he do?

Now we know that Peyton Manning felt a responsibility to his university, coaches, teammates, and fans that he would stay for his senior year and play. It was just the right thing to do. **How did he make that decision?**

Once your priorities in life are stated, it is much easier to make choices that are really in line with the type of life you have decided to live.

The road you choose will make you the type of person you will become. Our choices make the type of life we are going to live!

Peyton Manning stated his priorities for living life are as follows:

1. **God**
2. **Family**
3. **Friends**
4. **Football**

Now I am not a big fan of football, but I know many guys think football is everything. They follow all the players and their playing statistics and keep up-to-date on who is injured and who is the replacement. They watch every game and, sometimes, three games at the same time. Some even play fantasy football. Today, everything is about sports and, particularly, football. Today, many sports figures are idolized.

Peyton Manning was a great college quarterback, and many think he should have won the Heisman Award. He has gone on to be an outstanding professional quarterback and, as a team leader, has won the Super Bowl twice. He is also an outstanding person, as reflected by how he lives his life. He makes his decisions based on his Big Four lifetime priorities. **God is first in his life**. I am sure Peyton talked with God about his decision to play for UT in his senior year rather than sign up with the NFL.

I am sure it is difficult for many young football fans to think that football is not the top priority in his life. I am sure it is more difficult for them to understand it is priority number four in his life. They might also find it unusual to see that God is number one in his life.

I took a hard look at my life and rationalized that my job had to be number one priority in my life because if I did not have my job, I could not support my family. I know now this was not sound thinking. **There is a better way. God should have been first in my life. Be all that you can be**.

There is a saying:

"What lies behind us and what lies in our future fails in comparison to what lies within us."

This is called our untapped potential.

With God's Word, God's grace, God's plan, and God's help, you can learn how to tap your full potential and live the type of life God has for you. God will show you a better way to live your life. God has a plan for you.

Caution: In Physics, it is said "for every action, there is an opposite and equal reaction." It is the same when one makes a choice. For every decision, there is a consequence. **You can choose your decision, but you cannot choose the consequence.**

CHAPTER 3

You Are the Lead in Your Life's Story

Being a born-again Christian, I have delighted at the stories found in *Our Daily Bread*. It is a small book with a different story each day that makes a point followed by God's Word in scripture. *Our Daily Bread* ties God's Word in scripture to real problems we encounter in our lives and provides the wisdom for the best direction for us. *Our Daily Bread* is free for the asking, and I highly recommend this book. Salvation too is free for the asking. Salvation offers entrance to God's kingdom in Heaven and eternal life. It is free because Jesus paid the price of admission by dying on the cross for our sins.

> *"For God so loved the world that he gave his one and only Son, that whoever believes in him shall not perish but have eternal life"* (John 3:16).

(Note 3-1) "When actors and actresses make a movie, it's the director who sees the 'big picture' and the overall direction. Actress Marion Cotillard admits she didn't understand everything the director was doing in one of her recent films. She said, 'I found it very interesting to allow myself to be lost, because I knew I had this amazing guide. . . . You abandon yourself for a story and a director that will make it all work'" (note 3-2).

If God is the first priority in your life, then you should let God direct your life. He knows the big picture. Let God bless your life and show you His plan for you.

A few years ago, there was a popular bumper sticker for cars that said "God is my copilot."

If God is your copilot, you are in the wrong seat! Move over, and let God be the pilot in your life. Let God direct your life.

> *"So do not fear, for I am with you;*
> *do not be dismayed, for I am your God.*
> *I will strengthen you and help you;*
> *I will uphold you with my righteous right hand."*
> (Isaiah 41:10)

Sometimes, bad things happen in our lives, and we question if it is best for us and if God is really directing our lives. We question our faith in God.

Life is made up of the highest mountaintops and the lowest valleys. Some people blame God when they are in a valley and do not understand the total picture of God's plan for them. God might be testing your faith. He might be making you stronger.

When Paul was in prison, he had the opportunity to witness to many of the prisoners and bring them the grace of God that is Salvation through Jesus Christ and eternal life, in His Kingdom. Paul also used the time in prison to write many of the books in the Bible. Paul wrote the books, but it was at God's direction and God's Word. Paul did not question why God let that happen to him; he just used the time to do God's work.

It is human nature to take the credit when you are on the mountaintop due to favorable situations. People have a tendency to blame God when things don't go their way and take credit for themselves when they are on that mountaintop. If they get a promotion, they pat themselves on the back and feel good about what **they** have accomplished. They normally don't thank God for making it happen. If they are fired or laid off from work due to a decrease in the workforce, they blame God.

Remember, when God closes one door in your life, He opens another. If you concentrate on the closed door, you might not even see the open door and the new opportunity God has for you.

I have a saying: "**Sometimes, human nature isn't very human.**" Wars are an example of this, but there are so many other examples. With God at the center of your life, you should strive to act differently than most people. Show respect to others. Live your life by the Golden Rule to treat others as you would like to be treated. Also live your life by the Ten Commandments. Study God's Word in the Bible. It will make you a better person.

I went to Sunday School when I was in the fourth grade, and the teacher gave us an assignment. She wanted us to select a scripture from the Bible, read it to the class, and explain what it meant to us and why we selected it. I was overtaken by fear. I was very shy and did not have the confidence to do this. I was not a good reader—particularly, reading out loud to a group. I could, and should, have asked my mother for help, but I decided to just ignore the problem and hoped it would go away.

The next Sunday morning, I just hoped my parents would sleep in and not go to church, but they did wake up and wanted us to go. I told them I was not feeling well, and they let me stay home. I should have faced my fear and taken the challenge head on. I would have been stronger for conquering my fear rather than letting my fear conquer me. I am sure Satan had a hand in that. I was listening to Satan rather than God.

During my first marriage, I did not go to church on Sunday and was not a Christian. I was baptized when I was very young and tried to live a good life, so I thought, for this reason, I would have eternal life in Heaven. But I was wrong. The only way to eternal life is through Jesus by asking for the wonderful gift of Salvation.

> *"For God so loved the world that he gave his one and only Son, that whoever believes in him shall not perish but have eternal life"* (John 3:16).
>
> ———•◦•———
>
> *"Jesus answered, 'I am the way and the truth and the life. No one comes to the Father except through me. If you really know me, you will know my Father as well. From now on, you do know him and have seen him"* (John 14:6–7).

"Jesus said to her, 'I am the resurrection and the life. The one who believes in me will live, even though they die; and whoever lives by believing in me will never die. Do you believe this?" (John 11:25–26). Yes, I do believe this statement – What is being said is, if you die in the flesh, but believe in Jesus and ask Him for Salvation, your spiritual life will live in God's Heavenly Kingdom for eternity.

I would do home improvement jobs on Saturday and Sunday— also called "honey-do-jobs." I liked doing these jobs as it provided a sense of accomplishment I did not get in my career.

After my divorce, I met a wonderful lady named Susan. When I talked to Susan about my life, I told her I lived my life by most of the Ten Commandments and the only one I did not adhere to was keeping the Sabbath holy as a day of rest. Susan told me there were other commandments I did not adhere to such as having only one God. She said, on Sunday, I worshiped the "home improvement god." She was right, but I did not look at it that way.

Remember, we don't know what we don't know. There is so much to learn! Open up your mind and heart, and let God bless your life.

> *"The simple believe anything, but the prudent give thought to their steps"* (Proverbs 14:15).

There is an abundant wealth of information in the Bible. God's Word can help us with the decisions we face every day.

The Bible is the truth of God!

CHAPTER 4

What Special Gifts Were You Given by God?

Some people have many gifts and can do just about anything. Everyone has some gifts that makes them unique. All these gifts were given by the grace of God. This Bible scripture tells us that good gifts come from God.

> *Every good and perfect gift is from above, coming down from the father of heavenly lights, who does not change like shifting shadows.* (James 1:17)

One of my son-in-laws has a great aptitude for sports. I love snow skiing and have skied for many years. For me, it took lots of time, falls, and lessons to learn to ski. I taught my son-in-law how to ski, and he was a natural. Whatever I told him to do, he could just do it.

Most sports have basic rules. In snow skiing, one is to keep your weight on your downhill ski and keep your uphill ski in front of your downhill ski. If you don't do this, your skis will cross and you will fall. I told him this, showed him once, and he just did it. He was up skiing the more advance runs in two days. It is not that I am a great teacher, but rather he has a God-given gift for sports. That is a gift I do not have.

Who are you? What are your God-given special gifts? What do you enjoy doing when relaxing? Do you like team sports or individual sports? Do you have lots of friends or just a few close friends? What does your mother and father do for a living? Do you like to spend a lot of time alone or with lots of friends? Do you like to read a lot, spend time watching TV alone, or do you like group activities?

Everyone gets a tool box with special gifts when they are born. The tool box is filled with different tools that are gifts, depending on the person. Many of the gifts will be inherited from your mother and father. This is normally a good thing, but it could be something that puts up a red flag. It is said we spend our lives "living up to our parents" or "living down our parents' actions."

God has given all people the ability to make their own decisions. Sometimes, decisions are affected by Satan who will have a negative effect on our lives. A parent might have an addictive tendency. They might drink a lot and cannot control that desire. Their children might have this same desire. If so, the children should recognize they have that desire and ask God's help to keep them away from alcohol and other drugs.

Some people have the gift to make friends easily. Some have a gift for communicating. They are very good at talking and giving great speeches. They can be very convincing, and many are great at selling products or ideas.

Some people are really good with numbers. I was making a presentation to a group, and one lady told me, "You really make those numbers dance." It was a compliment, but numbers are not for everyone. Financial analysis was one of the greatest tools of the 20th century to help businesses become more profitable. Math is not for everyone, but if it is your gift, talk to your parents and God and follow His lead.

One of my daughters did not like math in school. It was difficult for her, and she did not get good grades. After she was married, she became great with their home finances. She was great at finding specials, budgeting expenses, working on retirement, and financing their home. She could do it all. She could relate to the actual application of the math. It was more than just numbers. It was their personal reputation to make sure they met their financial obligations.

It took me most of my life to fully understand myself. I have a type A personality, and therefore, I am a very assertive or aggressive person. I am also a very detailed person. I learned later in life that my type A personality says "go ahead and do something now," but my high D personality, for detail, says "take time and check it out in detail." This produces a situation that makes me question my decisions, and therefore, I am indecisive when making decisions. This is especially true when dealing with new information. This also makes me lack confidence in many of my decisions.

I am an introvert. Some people think this means I do not like people. That is not true. I am not a social butterfly as I prefer a few close friends. The word *introvert* means I am a person who makes their decisions through internalizing the objective information to arrive at a decision.

An extrovert is a person who talks to other people about their decisions, and after listening to their friends, then they make their decision. It will work, providing you talk to the right people, such as parents, grandparents, and God. Providing you really listen to your parents, they have a lot of good advice. Again, I did it my way. I should have listened to my parents on some of my big decisions. I should have prayed to God for the wisdom to make the right decisions for myself.

In the 1940s and 1950s, there was a very popular singer named Frank Sinatra who made the song "My Way" very popular. The song also represents the way I looked at my life. **But I have learned there is a better way.**

The Lyrics, written by Paul Anka for Frank Sinatra, of the song are as follows (note 4-1):

"And now, the end is near;
And so I face the final curtain.
My friend, I'll say it clear,
I'll state my case, of which I'm certain.

I've lived a life that's full.
I traveled each and every highway;
And more, much more than this,
I did it my way.

Regrets, I've had a few;
But then again, too few to mention.
I did what I had to do
And saw it through without exemption.

I planned each charted course;
Each careful step along the byway,
And more, much more than this,
I did it my way.

Yes, there were times, I'm sure you knew
When I bit off more than I could chew.
But through it all, when there was doubt,
I ate it up and spit it out.
I faced it all and I stood tall;
And did it my way.

I've loved, I've laughed and cried.
I've had my fill; my share of losing.
And now, as tears subside,
I find it all so amusing.

To think I did all that;
And may I say—not in a shy way,
'Oh no, oh no not me,
I did it my way.'

For what is a man, what has he got?
If not himself, then he has naught.
To say the things he truly feels;
And not the words of one who kneels.
The record shows I took the blows—
And did it my way!
Yes, it was my way."

With God as the number one priority in your life, the best thing is to read God's Word in the Bible and pray to God for direction. There is so much wisdom in the Bible that applies directly to today's problems and solutions to our daily life. This can really make your decisions clearer.

I am constantly learning about myself, and I am much more secure and confident in who I am than when I did it **"My Way."**

CHAPTER 5

My Family Background

In order to understand the decisions I made, one needs to understand my upbringing and family background. It is said up to the age of twelve, we learn 80 percent by what we see. Parents can tell their children what to do, but it is what children see their parents do that really teaches them.

I was born in January 1945, and World War II was still going on. We lived in a small two-bedroom home in Glendale, a town in Southern California. As our family grew, my parents added a third bedroom to that house. When I was nine years old we moved to a large four-bedroom home also in Glendale.

My parents were Methodists and had met at the Methodist Church in Chicago. My mother's father was an electrician and had a good job during the depression. My father's father was a postman. He was a farmer who lost his farm in Iowa in the depression. He came to Chicago to get a job that would be protected as he thought the same depression that hit the farmers would also come to the city, and it did. It was the Great Depression.

As a young man, my father decided to move to California for a better life. He did not have a lot of money, so he rode the rails out to California. He rode on box cars of trains like a hobo. He was very adventuresome. He saw the potential of aviation and went to a two-year aeronautical school, Curtis Wright, and became an aeronautical engineer. After graduating from school, he went back to Chicago to marry my mother, and they returned to California to make their home and raise a family. My father was not in the service as he was needed to support the war effort as an aeronautical engineer.

I had a brother who was three years older and a sister who was three years younger. We were not close as children. My sister had a love of horses as many young girls do. She won a number of ribbons for her riding in competition. She did not have very many friends that I recall. My brother was a super introvert who read and studied a lot. He earned excellent grades but did not have many friends. I can only remember one friend he had in high school. The friend drove a 1958 Chevy that was a real cool car for the time. My brother and his friend worked together on scientific experiments.

One day, my brother wanted to show me a bomb he had made using black gun powder and a battery-powered control switch to set it off. He had it wired up with a twenty-foot cord so he was far enough away when it went off. When he pushed the ignition switch, the bomb did not go off. He asked me to go and look at it. I went over, stood over the bomb, and looked down at it. I thought to myself that was not safe and backed away from the bomb. In just a few seconds after I stepped back, the bomb went off. It shot flames about four feet in the air. If it had gone off when I was looking down over the bomb, I could have lost my sight. I was stupid to do what he told me to. Now I know God has blessed my life and protected me.

My father was a good and honest man, but he was also very controlling of everything his two sons did. He would not let my brother buy a car when he was old enough but instead gave him the old family car. Cars were very important in California, and every boy wanted their own car so they could fix it up their way. It was like a statement of who they were. My father was also very critical of everything we did as boys. He was a perfectionist, and nothing was good enough for him. As the years went by, his critical nature affected our self-worth and self-confidence. My mother would say, "He is a good man, and he is just trying to help."

Sometimes in life, we have fathers who hurt us or disappoint us, and they do not realize the impact of their comments. That is when we should look toward our Heavenly Father who loves us.

I was not a good student in school. In fact, I had to repeat the second grade. Later in life, I found out I was dyslexic. Dyslexia is a learning disability that makes reading and learning very difficult. I did fairly well in math, but spelling and reading comprehension were a real challenge for me. To make things more difficult, the school system in Southern California decided not to teach the phonics system but rather spelling by memorization. This also made learning difficult for me.

Because I was doing well in math, I took algebra in the ninth grade. I still remember the teacher's speech the first day of the class. He said, "You have been learning to add, subtract, multiply, and divide for the last eight years, and you still have not mastered it. How am I supposed to teach you algebra in one year? This is hopeless!"

The teacher was very negative, and I was defeated before I even started. It was reflected in my grade as I got a low C in the class. If he had just said "You have been learning to add, subtract, multiply, and divide for eight years, and now, we are going to replace some of the numbers with letters to solve for the unknown letters," that I can understand. Later, I took advanced algebra in college and got an A. The college professor was excellent—a very positive professor. He also taught me many good life rules to live by.

During your life, you will find good teachers and good bosses, but you will meet ones you do not admire. You can learn what to do and what not to do with your life, but remember, God is the best teacher of all. His lessons are in the Bible in many valuable stories.

When I turned sixteen, I got my driver's license. That was the day of freedom. I studied for the license exam a lot to make sure I passed. I read each question to make sure I understood it correctly. That was a freedom day. Now I wanted a car.

My father said if I wanted a car, I would have to get a job and earn the money. My first job was a summer job in a very small Italian restaurant as a dishwasher. My mother used her car in the morning and would let me use it to go to work at night. I worked very hard and was promoted to pizza cook. Soon, I could cook any item on the menu. I worked from three in the afternoon until one in the morning. It was even later on the weekends—normally, until three in the morning. We got really busy when the bars closed for the night. I earned a dollar per hour and worked six days a week. At the end of the summer, I had saved over a thousand dollars. I had worked a lot overtime.

With money in hand, I asked my father if I could buy a car. He said I needed a regular job to support owning a car. After all, gas was twenty-five cents a gallon. He did pay my insurance, and for a teenage son, that can cost a lot. I did not really appreciate that until later in life, when I had to buy insurance for my daughters. I got a job working at WT Grant Co. as a cashier/sales/stock boy. I did not like the retail work as it was slow and boring compared to restaurant work. I only worked on Sunday, and they paid time and a half on Sundays. I was in the money for a dollar and fifty cents an hour.

In 1962, I found a 55 Chevy convertible in rough condition. The owner had installed new black-and-white seat covers, a new black convertible top, a three-speed shifter on the floor, and a corvette steering wheel. Cars were king in California. This one still had the two-tone paint in white and tomato soup color, and it needed some body work. I bought the car for three hundred thirty-five dollars, cash. I had it painted a blue-green color and added chrome reverse wheels. It was a sweet machine. The seller told me it had a corvette engine in it, but later, I learned that was not to be true.

I made some really stupid decisions in those days, but they did not cause me a "lot" of pain. Now I know it was God looking after me. Here are a few examples.

When I was thirteen years old, transistor radios became popular, and I had to have one. My father took me to a store in downtown Los Angeles, some distance from our home, and I bought my first small transistor radio. It was a bright red-orange color with a black leather cover and ran on AA batteries. It was small and portable and made by Realtone. I saw one in an antique store the other day, and it brought back a lot of good memories. This was in 1958, and rock and roll was just getting started.

I showed the radio to a friend, and he wanted to know where I got it. I told him it was on Broadway in downtown Los Angeles. He wanted to go see the store and look at the other radios available. We talked about taking the bus downtown. The bus driver said he could give us transfers, and that would allow us to take the bus right to the store. This was not really smart considering our ages.

That night, I was having dinner with my family. My mother asked me what we did that day, and I told her. She was very upset I went to Los Angeles without asking permission or any discussion. She said it was not safe for us to do that. We did not see the danger, but she knew better. She said if someone had called her and told her I was in Los Angeles, she would not have believed them.

When I had my driver's license, I had my freedom and more opportunities to make stupid decisions. My friend and I were driving down in the Long Beach area and saw the Long Beach Airport. There was a sign about flying to Catalina Island. We talked about it and thought we would check into it. It was very reasonable, and we could go over and fly back the same day. We had the money, so why not go for it? The airplane was a seaplane, and we would take off from the Long Beach Airport and land in the water at Avalon on Catalina Island. On the return trip, we would take off from the water and land at the Long Beach Airport. That would be a fun trip since neither of us had ever flown before. We went for it.

When we arrived at the island, we were told we would only have one hour, and since it was the last return flight, we better be on time if we were going to return that day. We did make the return trip and all was fine—we thought. At dinner that night, I was asked the same question— "What did you do today?"—and I was grounded.

I was very fortunate I never ran into any real problems even though my decisions were not always the brightest ideas. My life has been blessed.

While in high school, I was still having difficulty with grades and took auto shop and art to help increase my GPA. I was just drifting along with no real goal. In 1963, I graduated high school with a graduating class of 400 students, and I was number 200—right in the middle of the class. Mr. Average! I was eighteen years old.

To make good decisions that will help improve your life, you have to have a plan and a goal. When I graduated from college, I was told by one of the professors that students who graduate with a goal achieve 70 percent more than those who do not have a goal or a plan.

If you don't have a goal, it is like taking a trip and not knowing where you are going. How do you know when you get there?

Establishing those goals can be done by talking to your parents and asking God for direction.

CHAPTER 6

The Four Most Important Choices of Your Life

What are the Big Four? What are the four biggest and most important choices you will make during your lifetime?

That question takes serious consideration for sure.

Some people just let life happen to them. They go with the flow. Others take a lot of time considering their choices and decisions and make sure they are in line with their goals and God's plan. Here is what I think the four most important decisions one will make in their lifetime are:

1. **Will you make God the most important part of your life?**
2. **What will you do for your vocation, and what type of education will you need for your vocation?**
3. **Who will you choose to marry, start a family, and live with for the rest of your life?**
4. **Will friends be an important part of your life?**

> *"The simple believe anything, but the prudent give thought to their steps"* (Proverbs 14:15).

I will discuss all four of these choices in detail. They are so very important as they will affect your entire life.

Today is the Information Age.

There are so many voices today—who do you listen to?

There is the internet with lots of good information and some not-so-good information. We are bombarded with e-mails constantly about advertising, stories, jokes, and news, including local, national, and international. There is social media with information about what is the popular direction to take when you have to make a decision.

What is popular in today's culture can lead you in the wrong direction.

When seeking help with making decisions, you should talk with the people who love you. Seek wisdom from the Bible and, directly, by asking God for help. Talk with your parents and your grandparents as they also love you. Talk with teachers and counselors who really know you.

When talking with friends, make sure you are careful with their advice as many teens and young adults have been misdirected by their friends. They might tell you what they want you to do, but they are your age and do not have the wisdom, knowledge, or long-term perspective that others have. Sometimes, your friends have ulterior motives in giving you misleading information regarding your decisions. **They do not have the wisdom God has; nor do they have God's love, mercy, and grace.**

"Do not conform to the pattern of the world,
but be transformed by the renewing of your mind.
Then you will be able to test and approve what
God's will is—his good,
pleasing, and perfect will" (Romans 12:2).

———•••———

"1 Blessed is the one
who does not walk in step with the wicked
or stand in the way that sinners take
or sit in the company of mockers,
2 but whose delight is in the law of the LORD,
and who meditates on his law day and night.
3 That person is like a tree planted by streams of
water,
which yields its fruit in season
and whose leaf does not wither—
whatever they do prospers.
4 Not so the wicked!
they are like chaff
that the wind blows away.
5 Therefore the wicked will not stand in the
judgment,
nor sinners in the assembly of the righteous.
6 For the LORD watches over the way of the
righteous,
but the way of the wicked leads to destruction."
(Psalm 1:1–6)

Trust in God, and ask Him to give you directions for your life.

CHAPTER 7

Choice Number One:
The Most Important Choice
You Will Ever Make

Will you make God the most important part of your life? God should be the number one priority in your life. I did not take Jesus into my heart and ask Him to forgive my sins until later in life. To be exact, I was sixty-eight years old. My life was not moving in a positive direction. I was divorced after forty years of marriage, and I was all alone. I did a lot of reading to see what went wrong with my life and my marriage. I came to realize I was missing God in my life but did not really know which way to turn or what to do.

I did not consider myself a "nonbeliever" as I believed there was a God who created Heaven and Earth—such a beautiful place to live. Just look around on a beautiful spring day or look at the stars on a clear night. See a sunrise or a sunset. The beauty is everywhere. There is so much beauty it could not have happened by accident. I had a problem with understanding the logistics of God. How could God listen to everybody in the world and know their needs and wants? It just did not seem possible. Now I understand it is possible because with God, all things are possible.

> *"Jesus looked at them and said, 'With man this is impossible, but with God all things are possible'"* (Matthew 19:26).

School systems teach the "theory" of evolution where man developed from a lower life form over thousands of years. I believe the Bible because it is God's Word and tells us the story of creation.

If the theory of evolution was even possible, why did it only take place on planet Earth? Why is Earth the only planet to have the right atmosphere and climate conditions for humans? Why don't the other planets in our solar system have the same beauty as Earth? It is because that is how God created it—**just as the Bible says**.

Many people think because the Bible was written by man, it is not the Word of God. The Bible contains sixty-six different Books written by forty different authors over a period of one thousand five hundred years. **It is God's Word**! I know in my heart this is true because it is such an incredible book with so much history, wisdom, and knowledge contained in God's Word.

Sometimes, there are things about life that people will try to prove such as there is no God. They believe in Darwin's theory of evolution, where man evolved from a lower life form such as the chimpanzee. This is just a theory. When Columbus sailed to America in 1492, the popular theory was the world was flat and a boat would just fall off the earth if it sailed far enough. Now we know this is not true as the world is round.

We know what the Bible tells us about the creation of the earth, and it is not a theory. The Bible has over **two thousand five hundred** prophecies of what will happen in the future, and over **two thousand** have been proven to be true at this time. The remaining **five hundred** will come true in the future. Some when the Lord Jesus returns to the earth as clearly stated in the Bible.

In reflecting on my life, I have learned a lot of what I had done or did not do was from what I had learned from my father. He did not tell me to do these things, but I learned by watching what he did or did not do. He was an honest man and did not lie. He did not chase women or use tobacco products, alcohol, or any other drugs. My parents were Methodists and did go to church on Sunday, but we never prayed before a meal to thank God for His blessings.

My father never showed affection to my mother in front of us children. He never kissed her, he never put his arm around her, and he never would open the car door for her. When he came home after a long day of work, he would just criticize her about what she had done during the day. Up to the age of twelve, we learn 80 percent of what we know by what we see. It is mostly visual learning and acting out what we have learned. Unfortunately, I would follow that type of activity. The Bible tells us a better way—a much better way.

Several years after my divorce, I met a lovely lady, Susan. I admired Susan as God was the center of her life. I started going to church with Susan. She was saved when she was eleven years old and studied God's Word in the Bible and attended church regularly for her entire life.

Susan and I had a great time together, going on dates and talking about the future. She had a big decision to make. She had told one of her sisters she would never marry again unless she met someone who was a Christian—a Christian who really lived his faith.

I told Susan I wanted to be more like her as I admired her strong faith in the Lord. She said, "No, you should strive to be more like Jesus." I thought, "Wow, that is a big request." But I knew she was correct.

I was baptized in the Methodist Church and had lived an honest life, but I had never been saved. I had never turned my life over to Jesus and strived to live sin free and follow Jesus as my Lord and Savior. Susan's family reminded her of her pledge not to marry a person who was not a Christian. What should we do?

> *"For, 'Everyone who calls on the name of the LORD will be saved'"* (Romans 10:13).

Susan and I turned to Pastor Jim at our church to discuss our situation. I told him I had read a pamphlet on the Book of John. He asked me if I believed what I had read, and I told him I did. He asked me if I wanted to accept Jesus Christ as my Lord and Savior at that time. I told him I was not sure and I thought there was supposed to be a sign from God. I should have known **that** was my sign and my invitation. He said all right and did not push me to make a decision at that time. Pastor Jim prayed for Susan and me that I would find the way to come to Jesus. That was on a Wednesday afternoon.

That night, Susan and I went to church. Pastor Jim was praying, and he mentioned he had met with a nonbeliever and he prayed that person would not be led away from the church by Satan. I knew he was talking about me but did not use my name.

Susan was talking with a friend about my situation and that I was waiting for and expecting a sign. Her friend was concerned I might not understand the sign from God when it came. Susan said, "When God sends a sign to David, it will be something he will understand."

It was ten days after meeting with Pastor Jim on Sunday morning, June 30, 2013, that I decided to check my e-mails before going to pick up Susan for church. I opened the following e-mail from a good friend who did not know I was looking for a sign from God. The e-mail is below.

June 30, 2013

Absolutely great story! The end is surprising. This will give you chills.

Subject: The Pastor

After a few of the usual Sunday evening hymns, the church's pastor slowly stood up and walked over to the pulpit, and before he gave his sermon for the evening, he briefly introduced a guest minister who was in the service that evening.

In the introduction, the pastor told the congregation the guest minister was one of his dearest childhood friends and he wanted to have a few moments to greet the church and share whatever he felt would be appropriate for the service.

With that, an elderly man stepped up to the pulpit and began to speak.

"A father, his son, and a friend of his son were sailing off the Pacific Coast," he began, "when a fast approaching storm blocked any attempt to get back to shore. The waves where so high that even though the father was an experienced sailor, he could not keep the boat upright, and the three were swept into the ocean as the boat capsized."

The old man hesitated for a moment, making eye contact with two teenagers who were, for the first time since the service began, looking somewhat interested in his story.

The aged minister continued with his story. "Grabbing a rescue line, the father had to make the most excruciating decision of his life: to which boy would he throw the other end of the lifeline? He only had seconds to make the decision.

"The father knew his son was a Christian, and he also knew his son's friend was not. The agony of his decision could not be matched by the torrent of the waves.

"As the father yelled out 'I love you, son!' he threw the lifeline to his son's friend. By the time the father had pulled the friend back to the capsized boat, his son had disappeared beneath the raging swells into the black of night. His body was never recovered."

By this time, the two teenagers were sitting up straight in the pew, anxiously waiting for the next words to come out of the old minister's mouth.

"The father," he continued, "knew his son would step into eternity with Jesus, and he could not bear the thought of his son's friend stepping into eternity without Jesus. Therefore, he sacrificed his son to save his son's friend.

"How great is the love of God that He should do the same for us. Our Heavenly Father sacrificed His only begotten Son that we could be saved. I urge you to accept His offer to rescue you and take a hold of the lifeline He is throwing out to you in this service."

With that, the old man turned and sat back down in his chair as silence filled the room.

The pastor again walked slowly to the pulpit and delivered a brief sermon with an invitation at the end. However, no one responded to the appeal.

Within minutes after the service ended, the two teenagers were at the old man's side.

"That was a nice story," politely stated one of them. "But I don't think it was very realistic for a father to give up his only son's life in hopes that the other boy would become a Christian."

"Well, you've got a point there," the old man replied, glancing down at his worn Bible. A big smile broadened his narrow face. He once again looked up at the boys and said, "It isn't very realistic, is it? But I am standing here today to tell you that story gives me a glimpse of what it must have been like for God to give up His Son for me.

"You see, I was that father, and your pastor is my son's friend."

This was the first time I ever received an e-mail about Salvation, and I have never received a similar e-mail since that date. This is truly amazing to me. I know this was the work of God.

This was the sign I was looking for!

Sailing is my passion. I grew up in Southern California and have owned three sailboats. I learned to sail in the waters off Southern

California mentioned in this e-mail. I could really relate being offered the lifeline to Salvation by the Lord Jesus Christ. I was not sure what to do, so I looked on the internet, as funny as that might sound. I found the prayer and prayed a number of times.

> Dear God, I am a sinner and need forgiveness. I believe Jesus Christ shed His precious blood and died for my sins. I am willing to turn from sin. I now invite Christ to come into my heart and life as my personal Savior.

That was all I needed. When I went to pick up Susan, she saw my glassy eyes and said, "What happened?" When I just smiled with tears in my eyes, she said, "You got your sign." I smiled and said yes, and she read the e-mail.

When we got to church that morning, we went to see Pastor Jim to tell him the good news. He was pleased and congratulated me on my decision.

The sign that I received from God was very direct and could not be missed. Signs are not always that direct or timely. We have to have patience because God answers us on his time schedule and not on our schedule. Now I know one does not need a sign to ask for the gift of Salvation

Almost instantly, calm came over me. It was as if I was not really alone anymore. I understand now the Holy Spirit had entered my body and was there to help me make the right decisions. It was wonderful, and I had truly wished I had found Salvation many years earlier. How different my life might have been.

> *"What we have received is not the spirit of the world, but the Sprit who is from God, so that we may understand what God has freely given us"* (1 Corinthians 2:12).

In the past, I thought I was going to go to Heaven because I was basically a good person. I lived by the Golden Rule to do unto others as I would want them to do unto me. I followed some of the Ten Commandments, or at least I thought I lived by most of them. I was baptized in the church at a very early age. My parents told me if I died, I would go to Heaven. I would not go to church on Sunday, and I would do home improvement projects. I have learned living a good life is not enough.

No one gets into Heaven for eternal life unless it is through our Lord Jesus Christ. It is stated in the Bible.

> *"Jesus answered, 'I am the way, the truth, and the life. No one can come to the Father except through me'"* (John 14:6).

Many people do not understand this fact. They think they will see Jesus on Judgment Day and they will be able to persuade Jesus they have lived a good life. That might be true, but that will not give you eternal life in Heaven as stated in the Bible. You must take Salvation by giving your life to Jesus and asking Him to forgive your sins. That is the only way to eternal life in Heaven. Only Jesus can forgive your sins. You just have to ask Him.

We know what we know, but we don't know what we don't know. There is so much we still have to learn. If we were alive during the time Jesus was alive and a 747 airliner landed, what would people think? There was so much the people of that time did not know, and there is so much we do not know today. We must have faith and know God has a plan for us and, we must trust God's plan for us.

Baptism in the river

On September 15, 2013, I was baptized in a river at our church's summer picnic. It was a wonderful feeling of peace and security. Baptism is an outward sign to show other believers I had been saved.

> *"So in everything, do to others what you would have them do to you, for this sums up the Law and the Prophets. 'Enter through the narrow gate. For wide is the gate and broad is the road that leads to destruction, and many enter through it. But small is the gate and narrow the road that leads to life, and only a few find it'"*
> (Matthew 7:12–14).

The narrow road and the narrow gate is the way to Jesus and Salvation. It is a narrow road because it is less traveled. So many people miss out on the love of God because they do not believe.

> *"My help comes from the LORD,*
> *The Maker of heaven and earth.*
>
> *The LORD will keep you from all harm—*
> *He will watch over your life;*
> *The LORD will watch over*
> *your coming and going*
> *both now and forevermore."*
> (Psalms 121:2, 7–8)

CHAPTER 8

Choice Number Two:
What Career Will You Choose?

When I was growing up, I tried the restaurant work and liked it. Normally, restaurants require a team effort, with everyone working together toward the same goal—a good guest experience. I also tried retail work and found it not as rewarding. What I did not really understand was there were so many other career choices I would have been better suited for than restaurant work.

In 1964, I was nineteen years old. During my first summer at Yosemite National Park, I decided to make a career of restaurant management. I also decided to attend the City College of San Francisco and major in hotel and restaurant management. One day, my parents visited me at the park to see how my summer was going. I told them I had made my decision to go to the city college and study restaurant management.

To say the least, my parents did not agree with my decision. My father was an engineer, and my mother wanted me to be an architect. When I was growing, up I was always building things out of blocks and drawing pictures of houses. When new homes were being built a block away from our home, I was up there inspecting the work and looking at the floor plan. My parents were right, and I should have listened to them. I should have been an architect.

I have learned I have a lot of my father's gift for engineering, and I have my mother's gift for art. Before making such a big decision in my life, I should have prayed to God and sought my parents' advice. Big mistake! My parents knew me better than I knew myself, and I should have listened to them. I was listening to a friend I only knew for a short time and did not know me that well. That was a big mistake. Again, I did it my way.

Number Five of The Ten Commandments states we should Honor Thy Mother and Father.

As I look back on the decisions I made and my rationale for those decisions, the picture is clearer now. I had been successful in the area of food preparation and food service. It was my comfort zone. I lacked self-confidence, so I wanted to stay in my comfort zone. I should have challenged myself to listen to my parents and find a more rewarding career path for myself.

Today, I am using the gifts from my parents as I enjoy painting in oils and find it very rewarding. When people see my painting, they comment, "You must have been an engineer." This is because I mainly paint realistic paintings with lots of detail and perspective and not modern style or abstract art.

Before going to the City College of San Francisco, I attended Glendale College for a year and a half. That was where I took advanced algebra from an excellent teacher. He taught me more than just algebra.

First, he said, "School is a full-time job and work is a full-time job, and you can't do justice to both at the same time. Something will suffer. Summer jobs are a great place to get experience and earn money."

Second, he said, "The best money you can spend is on your education. It will pay you many dividends during your entire career. **Once you have an education, it cannot be taken from you.**"

I took this advice 100 percent for myself and my children. I received an Associate Degree from the City College of San Francisco and a bachelor's degree from Cornell University. I am happy to say both of my daughters attended four-year universities and received their bachelor's degree. One of my daughters went on to receive her doctorate. I told both of my daughters the same philosophy about investing in one's education. They did listen to me.

In selecting a vocation you want to follow, make sure you know your strengths and weaknesses in the gifts you were given. Everybody has them. We have those areas we excel in, and we have those areas where we have difficulty. These are the gifts we were given when we were born. There are also tests to help a person find a job that is right for them.

In June of 1969, at the age of twenty-four, I had graduated from college and was starting to work. I was classified as "IA"—ready to be drafted. The Vietnam War was going on. I decided it would be better to go in as an officer for three years rather than an enlisted man for two years. When I applied for Officer Candidate School, they gave me an aptitude test, and it said I should be an electrician. My grandfather was an electrician, and my father used electrical and hydraulics as an aeronautical engineer. So it is said an apple does not fall far from the tree.

When I was considering enlisting in the Army's Officer Candidate School, I was told I would get my first choice for the training I would receive. The only problem was my choice had to be one of three areas of service. One was infantry, one was armory, and one was artillery. As I reviewed the three choices, I thought the safest place would be the artillery as I would be further away from the front line. At this time, the Vietnam War was going strong.

Many years later, when I was working in Myrtle Beach, I was negotiating with the owner of the restaurant we were leasing. We were talking, and he said he was in World War II. I asked him what area he was in, and he said artillery. I told him that was going to be my choice and asked him specifically what he did. He said he was a forward observer. He was across the front line in enemy territory to radio corrections to the artillery to ensure they hit their target. **Wow, my life has been blessed**.

Before we ended our meeting and discussion, I thanked him for his service to our country as I know freedom is not free. He seemed surprised and thanked me for recognizing his service to our country.

I was not drafted because President Nixon put in a lottery system. My lottery number was 251, and they stopped drafting that year at number 195. I was safe. At this time in my career I had just started with the Disney Organization after graduating from college. This was about eighteen months before the opening of Walt Disney World in Florida in October of 1971, and I did want to be a part of the experience.

As I reflect on my life, I realize it is our duty to serve our country. Freedom is not free, and many have paid the price with their lives. I think it is a duty and also a growing experience that helps one mature. I had an opportunity to go into the reserves. I could have signed up for the reserves and still had time for the opening of Walt Disney World in Florida. **Another missed opportunity.**

During my final semester at the City College of San Francisco, I was encouraged by Mrs. Hilda Watson Gifford, the first woman graduate of the Cornell School of Hotel Administration, to apply for a scholarship to attend Cornell University. Both programs were funded by The Statler Foundation, founded by the greatest hotelman for the first half of the 20th century, E. M. Statler. Mr. Statler believed in education for the hotel industry and established a foundation for that purpose.

My application to Cornell was rejected because of my poor grades in high school, even though my City College of San Francisco grades were mostly A's. Most of the students at Cornell were from prep schools and had excellent qualifications. Only after Mrs. Gifford talked with the dean of the Cornell School of Hotel Administration was I admitted. BUT, there is always a BUT. I was put on probation. If I did not get a 2.0 GPA the first semester, I would be invited to leave. They did not have much confidence in me, and the pressure was on me big time!

When I arrived at Cornell, it was on a Saturday afternoon and the admission office was closed, so I had to wait until Monday morning. I looked up my cousin who was also at Cornell the same time. He helped me get a place to stay until I could get in the dorms on Monday. He asked if I wanted to join his fraternity. I said I could not consider that due to the pressure to get good grades so I could take advantage of this wonderful opportunity. I felt like I owed it to myself, my parents, and Mrs. Gifford for believing in me.

Lesson: When making a life-changing decision, get the advice of people who love you—God, your parents, grandparents, and teachers who know you.

As I continued on with my education at Cornell, there were classes I liked and classes I did not like. Chemistry and economics were classes I did not care for. I liked my accounting classes, food facility engineering (designing restaurants), and my computer class. We all had to take a class about computers and computer programming, and this was in 1969. This was before any personal computers or Apple computers.

We programmed in the language of Fortran Four, a science programming language that was more complicated than basic computer language because everything had to be defined. The computer was an IBM 360. We had punch cards for the programs, and when we ran the punch cards through the computer, it took one hour to get the results. For my class project, I decided to make a program to run payroll and typed all the cards. After a number of refinements, the program worked. It seemed very natural to me. It was very logical in the way it all went together.

My instructor said he had a number of restaurant companies that were looking for someone like me and asked me whether I was interested. I had decided to take a job with Disney, working in their restaurant operations when I graduated. **I consider it a real missed opportunity** to take a job dealing with computers that was really suited for me. That was before personal computers, and it was the beginning of the tremendous growth of computers in business to increase productivity. **Again, I should have asked God and my parents for their advice. Again, I did it my way.**

That was a big mistake. You see, the job of restaurant operations is really a people game, and that is not my strong suit. You are making a lot of decisions one right after another. They are all people decisions and guest decisions. I am more of a "things person" and prefer working to solve problems, like computer programming, systems design, financial analysis, or restaurant design. A few years later, after graduating, I tried to move into restaurant design and financial analysis, but by that time, I was marked as a restaurant operations person.

Lesson: When deciding on a type of career and where to work, make sure you choose something that matches your strong qualities and get advice from people who love you—God, parents, grandparents, and teachers.

If you select a career in the field of work that you love, you never have to work a day in your life.

After two and a half years at Cornell, I did graduate—with distinction. I was in the top 10 percent of my class. Who would have guessed! Mr. Average did OK. **I know now nothing good happens without God, and I know His hand was on me and He has blessed my life.**

> *"Every good and perfect gift is from above, coming down from the Father of the heavenly lights, who does not change like shifting shadows"* (James 1:17).

Everyone does not have to go to college. One should select the type of career they want and then research the type of education and training required. There are a lot of good-paying jobs with good retirements that do not require a college education. Many students graduate from colleges and universities today and cannot find a job and cannot pay for their student loans.

If someone is good at working with their hands and that is their gift, it would be better to get the type of training for a specialized manufacturing job. Today, manufacturing is getting very "high tech" and requires the knowledge and use of computers. Many of these jobs pay better than college graduates earn. **It is not always about the money. It is getting the right fit for one's skill level that matches their God-given gifts.**

CHAPTER 9

Choice Number Three: Who Will You Marry?

This is really a big decision and should not be taken lightly. This will be the partner you will spend the rest of your life with. This will be the person you build a life and family with. When you meet the person you want to marry, there are all kinds of tests and theories on how to go about it.

Some of the date matching websites say you should marry someone with different and complimenting skills and characteristics. Other websites say you should marry someone with the same skills, likes, and characteristics. Which is right?

It has been said opposites attract. Two people who have different gifts and abilities do make a more complete person than two people with similar gifts and abilities. The more important consideration should be a strong agreement that the two people are going to tie the knot of marriage and they are totally committed to making it work—"Till death do us part." Many couples enter marriage with the idea that if it does not work, they will just get a divorce. If that is their attitude, they should not marry.

Let's take a look at the numbers.

1.   Fifty percent of all marriages end in divorce. In America, there is an average of three thousand divorces each day!

Unfortunately, mine ended that way after forty years of marriage.

2. The percentage of the population who are married is at the lowest point since they have been keeping records in the 1950s. Less than 50 % of all adults are married.

3. More people are living together who are not married. This is not against man's law, but it is certainly in violation of God's law and God's Word in the Bible as this is a sin.

4. "Marriages fail when expectations are not met." So simple, yet so true.

What should be considered?

1. You should marry a person who shares your faith in God and God's Word, allowing you to daily practice your faith together. In this way, you will most likely have very similar values and priorities for your life together as they will be based on the same faith.

2. Marriage is a contract with God. There is a man, a woman, and God. Marriage is a relationship like a triangle. The closer you get to God, the closer you get to each other.

3. Marriage is not about what you are going to get. It is about what you are going to give, which is everything.

4. Marriage is not a 50 percent and 50 percent union but rather a 100 percent and 100 percent union. Go into marriage with the mindset that you are going to give 100 percent to your partner.

5. The most important quality each person should have is a very high level of honesty and integrity.

6. You should enter marriage with the idea that no matter what happens, both of you are dedicated to making it work forever—till death do you part.

7. You need the ability to communicate openly about any subject.

8. Compromise is very important when two people have different views on decisions to be made. It is important to

be a good listener and consider the other person's side and their point of view

9. It is difficult to be objective when you are in love, so take your time and make sure your decision is one you can live with, till death do us part.

10. Seek advice from those who love you—God, your parents, your grandparents, and close friends who know you.

11. The woman is seeking love from her husband, and the man is seeking respect from his wife. The more he loves his wife, the more respect she gains and shows to her husband. In a good strong marriage, this is a positive circle of reinforcement.

12. What does the Bible tell us about love?

> *"Love is patient, love is kind. It does not envy, it does not boast, it is not proud. It does not dishonor others, it is not self-seeking, it is not easily angered, it keeps no record of wrongs. Love does not delight in evil but rejoices with the truth. It always protects, always trusts, always hopes, always perseveres. Love never fails"* (1 Corinthians 13:4–8).

There is so much wisdom in the Bible.

CHAPTER 10

Choice Number Four: Your Friends

Friends are a gift you give yourself. Real good friends are like GOLD, and you should protect your friendship with them.

I worked all over the country and in Japan for about a year and a half. I have worked with a lot of different people and for a lot of different people. As I moved on from one job to another, I would lose contact with my friends. This was unfortunate. Some of my friends were people who worked for me, and when I was no longer their immediate supervisor, the friendship evaporated.

I would start a new job and meet new people. Some I liked and admired, and some I did not like or admire. But I had to work with them and make the best of it.

As I mentioned, I am an introvert. I am more of a things person than a people person, but later in life, I realized the importance in staying in contact with friends and keeping friendships alive. **The Game of Life is a team sport.**

As a manager of people, I would focus on the results I was trying to achieve rather than the people. As a manager, one must develop the "want to" in the people they supervise so they will have the direction and the drive to accomplish the desired results.

The test of a really good restaurant manager is not how well their restaurant operates when they are in charge, directing the show, but how well the restaurant operates when they are not there!

Short story about friends and supervising people

While working for Walt Disney World, I would travel to a number of universities that offer a food service management program. We would hire some of the students to work at Walt Disney World for the summer and work as assistant supervisors in the restaurants. They would gain food service and supervisory experience. It was a very competitive program, and it was the way I started with Disneyland in the summer of 1968 at the age of twenty-three.

While interviewing students in the food service management program at the University of Denver, we would also talk with the professors about their programs. One professor shared the following story he would use to teach his students good leadership skills.

The professor told his class, "The final exam will be a week from Friday, and the term papers will be due on Wednesday of the same week."

Most students like to procrastinate when possible. They would concentrate on completing their term papers for the Wednesday deadline and then use Wednesday night and Thursday to "cram" for the final exam on Friday.

When the students showed up for class on Monday of the next week, the instructor made the following announcement. He said, "I have changed my mind. I will give you until Friday to turn in your term papers, AND I have decided to give you the final today!"

The students were outraged at the audacity of the professor. This was not fair. The professor said he was the one in charge, and it was not a group decision. He wanted to know what they had learned without "cramming" for the exam. This was his decision.

The following Monday, the professor handed out the results of the final exam. Eighty percent of the class failed the exam. They felt the professor was out of line to give them the exam at a different time when they could not study.

The professor asked some of the very verbal students what they thought of him for arbitrarily giving the final exam early.

One student called the professor a "real jerk," and the professor wrote that name on the blackboard at the front of the room for all to see. Now the rest of the students started giving even more names that were very descriptive and not very professional and cannot be used in this book or anywhere else for that matter. College students have a very large vocabulary of these types of words. In a short amount of time, the entire blackboard was filled with similar names for the professor.

Then the professor said, "Here is the real lesson. All of you are going to be in positions of leadership, and when you lead your people to believe one thing and then do something else, this is what they are going to think of you as a leader." Then he pointed at the names on the blackboard. The class became very quiet as they were deep in thought.

One student asked the question, "Now that we know the real lesson, can we retake the exam to get a better grade?" The professor stated, **"If I change your grade, you will not remember the lesson!"**
Now that lesson was a tough lesson to learn!

This story also applies to friends. When you tell your friends one thing and then do something else, they cannot count on your word and you have lost their trust. It can take years to earn a friend's trust, and it can be lost in one incident of a misunderstanding or dishonesty.

The right friends are like gold.

What makes a good friend? These are just a few of the qualities one should look for.

1. A friend should share your faith in God and live that faith every day.
2. A friend should have similar interests.
3. A friend should have the same value system as you do.
4. A friend should be supportive of you and strive to use good judgment in recommending what to do together.
5. A friend should never recommend actions that are dangerous or illegal. If a friend does, they are not a friend of yours.

6. If you move or go to college, you should strive to stay in touch with good friends. Today, this is much easier with social media.
7. Good friends are great when you are out of school and looking for a better or different job. Networking is a good tool that has been used to find many people new jobs or recommend someone for a job in a company where they work.
8. Honesty is very important with a true friend and everyone you come in contact with.

Some people will pretend to be your friends for personal motives and might not have your best interest in mind. That is why you should watch out for false friends.

> *"Do not be misled: 'Bad company corrupts good character'"* (1 Corinthians 15:33).

Caution: Sometimes, friends ask you to do stupid things in the name of testing your friendship.

During high school, when you are making more of your decisions, you might want to try new experiences. You might want to try a new sport, like scuba diving or surfing. Sometimes, one of your friends might try to talk you into trying the following: smoking, drinking beer or whisky, or taking drugs with very addictive qualities. These can lead to real trouble.

When I was growing up and in high school, the drug of choice was beer. We would drive around and see if we could get someone to go into a liquor store and buy us some beer because the legal age was twenty-one to purchase alcoholic beverages. Then we would drive around drinking the beer. Not smart. Not smart at all. Someone would say, "You are too drunk to drive." We would say, "I have to drive because I am too drunk to walk!"

Again, my life was blessed that we did not run into someone or kill someone. This type of activity was just plain stupid.

Friends might try to talk you into stealing the beer or cigarettes. This is when your life will really change. Remember you can choose your decisions, but you cannot choose the consequences of your decisions.

Most of the people in jail will tell you they thought they would never get caught or they are innocent of the crime. Some people will not take responsibility for their actions.

Should a friend of yours suggest any activity that is dangerous or illegal, just remember your priorities in life.

1. What would Jesus do?
2. Would my parents approve?

That is the test you should use.

Remember: It is so true that bad company corrupts good character.

And that is why a true friend is like gold.

The best friend you can have is God. This is because God loves you the most and wants only the best for you. If you have faith in God, He will give you hope and inspire your self-confidence. Remember, God has a plan for your life, and He will help you achieve that plan.

CHAPTER 11

How Did I Do on the Big Four Choices?

Now I will try to objectively see how I did with the Big Four choices I have listed and try to give myself a grade.

1.   Will you make God the most important part of your life?

I will have to say since I did not take Salvation until the age of sixty-eight, I failed this choice. God was not lost, I was lost.

I was not the spiritual leader of my family as a man should be. But I will have to say that **late is better than never**. I am so happy with my choice to ask Jesus for Salvation at the age of sixty-eight.

2.   What will you do for your vocation, and what type of education will you need for your vocation?

I should have been an engineer, accountant, or architect. I am more of a task-oriented person than a people person. I did get a good education, but I would have been more successful if I had selected a vocation such as accounting, computers, or restaurant design, all of which I did enjoy and were in line with my God-given gifts. Hindsight is always 20/20.

3. Who you will marry, start a family, and live with for the rest of your life?

My marriage ended in divorce after forty years; therefore, I would have to say I failed this choice. But there is a bright spot. We share two beautiful daughters who are happily married to wonderful husbands and have beautiful families that include four grandchildren.

It takes two people to make a marriage work, and if it does not work, both people should share the responsibility.

I will have to say divorce is the "death" of a relationship, and it is difficult on children even when they are adults.

I am a happier person now that I have found God's Word, and I am learning as much as I can. I have remarried and my wife and I share the same faith in God. She is much more knowledgeable in God's Word than I am, but I am learning a lot from her, from our church that we attend, and most importantly, God's wonderful Word in the Holy Bible.

God has blessed my life so many times.

4. Will friends be an important part of your life?

Friends are a very important part of one's life. I should have made an effort to keep in touch with the people I have worked with all over the country.

How did I do?

It is painful to review my life in these terms. If I was to give myself a grade, I would have to say it is only 25 percent based on a possible 100 percent. I only hope the teens and young adults can learn from my experiences to make better decisions. There is a better way with God in your life and you living God's plan for your life.

We should spend time looking forward and not backward as we cannot change the past. That's why we say **you cannot drive your car looking in the rearview mirror.**

CHAPTER 12

Call to Me

(Note 12-1) God is eager to communicate with His children. The Lord's words to Jeremiah extend to us as well: *"Call to me and I will answer you, and show you great and mighty things.* (Jeremiah 33:3). What we need to do is get ready to hear Him. Hearing from God is a learning process that takes time, but it is available to everyone who desires it. We don't have to have reached some high level of spiritual maturity. We don't have to have it all together, with all the struggles of our lives under control. He is available to us just as we are.

It is also important that we allow ourselves the freedom to listen expectantly for Him. During Jesus's ministry, He took time alone with His Father and told His disciples to do the same (Mark 6:31, 46). We too need a quiet place free from distraction. Once there, how do we know what we're hearing is truly from God?

Here are some questions you can ask yourself to determine if it is God speaking to you:

- Is it consistent with scripture?
- Is it consistent with the character of God?
- Does it lead to change or growth in your life?
- Does it lead to the restoration of relationships?
- Is there a sense of healing—release from past sin or pain?

- Is there a sense of peace, a lessening of anxiety, or contentment where once there was strife?
- Does it lead to conviction instead of guilt?

There is a distinct difference between the convictions of the Holy Spirit and the condemnation of the Devil because the two speak different languages. The characteristics of each should help you distinguish who is speaking. However, we sometimes mistake Satan's voice for God's because Satan's voice fits so well with our own distortions and misunderstandings about God and how we think He feels about us. But God speaks to us in a way that is completely different from the condemnation of Satan.

How can you tell the difference? Satan communicates in the following way:

- **Tone** - accusing, nagging, and mocking; generates fear and causes confusion.
- **Vague** - generates an overall sense of guilt, as if everything is wrong; creates feelings of hopelessness and weakness.
- **Discouraging** - attacks your self-confidence; tells you that you are weak and worthless.
- **Brings up the past** - replays your sin and shame; reminds you of your poor choices.
- **Rejecting** - produces the feeling that God has rejected you as unworthy and unholy. Portrays God as judge and you as a miserable sinner.
- **Isolating** - gives suggestions that cause you to withdraw from others.
- **Negative** - tells you the horrible way you feel is the way it is.

The conviction of the Holy Spirit is just the opposite:

- **Tone** - gentle, loving, imploring, and urges your return to Him.
- **Specific** - tells you to take a specific action in response to sin; freedom follows.

- **Encouraging** - says you can rely on His power, not your strength.
- **Releases you from the past** - tells you your sins are forgiven, never to be held against you.
- **Attracts** - generates an expectation of kindness, love, and a new beginning with His help.
- **Draws into fellowship** - sends others to minister to you in love, as well as sends you to others; speaks of His unchanging nature and steadfast love.
- **Truthful** - states the facts about you and God.

Use the list above as a guideline so you will be able to clearly hear God's responses as you share your heart with Him.

The Bible is clear about the fact that God actively pursues a personal relationship with His children. He delights in you and desires to bring restoration to the painful places in your life. He offers Himself as a refuge from fear and anxiety. He holds out His strength to those who are weak, and He longs to mourn with those who are broken. He is here for you—anytime you come.

He is gently calling, "Come with me."

(From *Our Daily Bread*, see notes 12-2.)

Many times, when I have wanted to make a different choice in my life, there was a "voice" in my head telling me I cannot do that as I am not good enough, smart enough, or deserving of such a gift. Now, when I hear that voice, I know it is Satan, and I will not listen to him.

> *"The thief comes only to steal and kill and destroy; I have come that they may have life, and have it to the full"* (John 10:10).

CHAPTER 13

Growing Pains

During my thirty-five-year career in multiunit restaurant operations, I moved around the country about every five to six years after spending fifteen years with the Disney Organization.

When my youngest daughter was a freshman in high school in Knoxville, Tennessee, I received an offer of a promotion. I was to move to Utah to the company headquarters to be the director of food service for forty plus company-operated restaurants.

As we moved around the country, I always tried to live in the areas with the best schools for the education of my daughters and the resale of our home. In Utah, I asked my coworkers where the best schools were and they indicated one particular area. They cautioned me not to move close to the Air Force base because the students there were from all over the country and they had a lot of problems. The truth of the matter was they were just like my daughter as she had moved a lot and lived in many areas of the country. There was a more diverse group of students at the military base.

When we moved to a suburb of Salt Lake City, we lived in an area that was highly concentrated with neighbors of a different religious belief—mainly, Mormons.

At school, my daughter was the target of students who tried to get her to change her religious beliefs. They asked her to go to church rallies after school. Then they would take her home, and they would go on to other student functions such as basketball and football games. She was brokenhearted to be excluded from their other school functions. This made her religious beliefs in Christ grow even stronger.

After spending two years in Utah, we let her return to Knoxville to live with her best friend's family and complete her senior year. She was very unhappy in Utah but managed to earn a 4.0 GPA from both high schools.

Utah was not a total loss as she learned she had her grandmother's gift for art and she found her love of snow skiing and became an excellent skier.

The early years

When we are very young children, our parents make most of the decisions in our lives. Sometimes, children younger than one year old will start to make their own decisions. If a child of one does not like the taste of a certain food, they just spit it out. That is a reactionary decision.

As one continues to grow up, they start to make a few of their own decisions. It is said up to the age of twelve, what we learn is 80 percent from what we see. That is why it is so important for parents to be good role models for their children. You can tell a child not to smoke, but if a parent smokes, it is normally a trait the child will copy. Children will also copy bad language, intimidations, bullying, racial discrimination, and other bad habits from their parents.

Children who live in homes where they are exposed to good qualities and good moral values tend to follow their parents' example. That is why two-parent homes, with a mother and father, are so important to bringing up the next generation.

Children of a good home environment are normally very happy at the "before school" years. They are very positive, always smiling, and have lots of self-confidence and tons of energy.

School years

School years can be fun as children can make lots of new friends. It can also be very difficult for some children who are in some way different from the other children. They can be excluded from a group just because they do not wear clothes that are considered "cool" by their friends. Children can be really mean and hurtful in their relationships. Some even start to bully other children. They can be called names with bad connotations, they can have their lunches stolen by bullies, or they can even get beat up by other kids. When children are called these names by their friends, the names stay with them in their mind and plays on their self-confidence.

High school years: the teenage years

In high school, teens seem to get more paranoid about who they are. There is a caste social system that develops, and some groups think they are better than the other teens. Some groups are the cheerleaders; some are the football players. Sometimes, it is a group of the teens who have a lot of money and the best clothes. In my high school, the letterman jacket was a big deal to move a person into more social acceptance by other teens.

To make the growing pains even more complex, this is the time when teens are starting to date and their hormones are changing their feelings and their appearance.

Sometimes, the teens use social media such as Facebook to bring negative comments toward specific teens. In some cases, it has resulted in the death of teens because the negative pressure was so great they decided to take their own life. This is a time when God can really help if they would just reach out, call on Him, and not listen to Satan!

Most parents set limits for students while they are in high school. This could include giving them jobs to keep their room clean, take out the trash, cut the lawn, wash the cars, cook, or wash the dishes. They set limits on where the student can go and when they should be home. This is not to punish their children but to keep them safe and develop some basic level of responsibility and work ethic for when they are in college or out in the working world.

Some students will rebel against their parents and tell them the other students don't have such jobs or restrictions. I remember a story of one parent who had set a curfew of ten in the evening for their son to be home on a week night. Their son got home after one thirty in the morning, and the father was waiting up for him. The father proceeded to discipline the son and take some of his privileges away from him. Their son went into a rage and said he was going to move out of his home because he could not stand all the rules and regulations. His father asked where he was going to go. Their son said he was going to go join the US Marine Corps. I am sure the Marines will provide an attitude adjustment.

Satan and the high school years

> *"The thief comes only to steal and kill and destroy; I have come that they may have life, and have it to the full"* (John 10:10).

Satan has a plan for our lives, but it is much different from the plan God has for us. Satan cannot stop God, but he will try to stop you from listening to God. Satan will try to steal your self-confidence, destroy your relationships, and kill everything that is good and positive in your life. When you hear that negative voice of Satan in your head, just tell yourself it is Satan and do not listen. God will empower you to fight off the curse of Satan. Listen to God and the Holy Spirit that is within you.

Some students will attack another student's religious beliefs. They will say it is not cool to believe in Jesus Christ and you should not be a believer. Stand firm on your belief in God, and do not waiver. God is your best friend and will stand by you always!

Some students who are not believers don't want you to be a believer. Many times they just don't know about God's Word; therefore, they are jealous of what you have. They want to make fun of your beliefs and try to get you to become a nonbeliever. They just don't know what they don't know. They are not educated in God's Word. A friend like this is no friend of yours. Stand firm on your belief in God as He will always stand firm for you!

The college years

The college years can offer new challenges that are not in the high school years. Mainly, students have more independence and therefore more personal responsibility, especially when they are living on campus. Individuals will handle this independence and responsibility differently depending on their level of maturity and family values.

The college structure establishes some of the rules that students must live by in order to stay in school and graduate. Therefore they are not really 100 percent on their own, but within the structure of the college guidelines, they are making most of their own decisions.

Some students will be attracted to the night life and the opportunity to party all the time. I have known many students who do not recognize the opportunity their parents are providing them with a college education, and they end up being forced to leave college due to bad grades. It truly is a missed opportunity!

Many of the college students are exposed to smoking, drinking, and sins of the flesh. These are dependent traits that can stay with them for their entire lives. Remember, **make responsible decisions, and take responsibility for your decisions.**

When young adults leave the church

College years are also a time when many young adults will leave the church. It is sad to say that 88 percent of students in Sunday school will leave the church by the time they are eighteen years of age, never to return. They really need Jesus in their lives to guide them and help them make the difficult decisions they face at this time in their lives.

What reasons do they give for leaving the church? (see notes 13-1)

- They simply wanted a break from church.
- Church members seemed judgmental or hypocritical.
- They moved to college and stopped attending church.
- Work responsibilities prevented them from attending.
- They moved too far away from church to continue attending.
- They became too busy, though they still wanted to attend.
- They didn't feel connected to the people in the church.
- They disagreed with the church's stance on political/social issues.
- They chose to spend more time with friends outside of the church.

There is an excuse for just about everything.

Many people use the excuse that they are too busy. The answer to that is simple. **We make time for what is important to us**. When people say they do not have time, they are really saying it is not important to them.

Many large universities have churches right on the campus. It is a great way to meet fellow students of the same faith.

These growing years can be very difficult if you listen to the negative talk of fellow students or the negative talk of Satan. Listen to the Holy Spirit and to God's Word. God loves you and wants to bless your life.

CHAPTER 14

Are You Ready to Vote?

Who should you vote for?

When you turn eighteen years old, you will have an opportunity to become a registered voter. America is a republic that is **"of the people, by the people, for the people."** Voting is an opportunity and a responsibility and should not be taken lightly. You should prepare yourself by becoming knowledgeable of the candidates and their views, platforms, and what their parties stand for. How should you do this?

I have talked to a lot of people, and this is what I hear as their reasons for picking a candidate:

1. I just vote for the party of the candidate that my parents are voting for.
2. I just vote for the candidate my brothers and sisters are voting for.
3. I just talk with my friends at school and vote the way they are voting.
4. My union tells me which candidate to vote for.
5. My boss tells me which candidate to vote for.
6. I listen to the candidate and pick the one that sounds the best.

Many soldiers have died fighting wars to keep America great and protect this right you have as an American citizen, and it should not be taken lightly.

Types of government

When America was founded, most of the world consisted of one type of government—the monarchy. There was a king or a queen who ruled the country. They were the absolute law of the land. They made all the laws and controlled the people as they wanted. People were born into a class. If their parents were famers, then they were expected to be famers. If their father was a silver smith, they were the same. If they were poor people, there was very little opportunity to move up the ladder and make a better life for their family. Some of the kings and queens were good to their people, and some were very demanding with lots of laws and lots of taxes to be used by the rulers of the country. Freedom and opportunity simply did not exist. We still have some monarchies in the world today.

Many of the people did not like the lack of freedom in Europe and wanted more freedom—particularly, the freedom to worship who and where they wanted. Religious freedom was the main freedom they were seeking.

The founding of America

America had a new form of government that was "of the people, by the people, for the people." The people would rule themselves. Founding Fathers did not know if this would work or not. It did work, and it would build the strongest and wealthiest nation in the world. The reason it worked was the basic structure that was put in place, with checks and balances so one person would not have all the power. The other reason it worked is because America has been "one Nation under God." God has blessed America.

Our Founding Fathers were very smart and put together a new form of government that would improve on the old system of a monarchy, with one absolute leader and people were locked into a class, a job, and a life of poverty. Today, some people do not recognize God and do not like any reference to God. They want to change America and have removed the reference to God from our schools, universities, and government buildings.

God has blessed America far more than our Founding Fathers could have ever imagined. We have less than 5 percent of the world's population, and we have 50 percent of the world's wealth. This happened because of the freedom and opportunity that was available to the people. That is why we are proud to say "God bless America" and God has blessed America.

The Founding Fathers were smart enough to know some people in government would try to gain more power, and therefore, they put in effective checks and balances to ensure that one area of the government would not try to rule the others. There is the executive branch with the president, the judicial branch with the Supreme Court, and the legislative branch with the Congress, consisting of the House of Representatives and the Senate. Congress is the voice of the people.

One check on the laws is the trial by jury. When one person has filed a suit against another person for a violation of the law concerning their rights, the actions of the people are being tested and the law is also being tested. If the jury finds that the law is not just and violates some of our freedoms as stated in the Constitution or Bill of Rights, the law is also on trial. This is the check on the Congress that makes the laws.

Many people do not realize the importance of the trial by jury and try to get out of serving on the jury. It is really an important part of testing the validity of the laws. We are a Nation of laws.

America is a capitalistic nation

Capitalism is the best form of government because it unlocks the potential of the people and therefore supplies the economic potential for our country.

Because of the freedom and opportunity in America, we have invented the light bulb, telephone, cell phone, airplane, internet, and GPS, just to mention a few of the contributions enjoyed by the entire world.

The measure of capitalism is sales, less labor cost, and product cost. The surplus is called *profit*, and profit is not a dirty word. To increase profits, the companies will use productivity to measure if they are making the maximum profit.

What is productivity? It is an objective measure of one business compared to a similar business in what they are producing. An example is the number of labor hours required to assemble a car on the production line.

When America was first founded, about 97 percent of all people were farmers, mostly producing food for their family and selling any surplus. Today, only 3 percent of the population are farmers. The industrial age and constant improvement in farming equipment and crops have allowed this to happen. Today, large farms have combines that use GPS to ensure the best way to harvest their crops.

In Socialism, the government makes most of the decisions, and with Communism, the government makes all the decisions and tells the people what to do. Therefore, creating a lack of freedom and motivation to get ahead in the development of personal wealth and happiness.

The political parties in America

There are basically two political parties in America today. There is the Republican Party and the Democratic Party. What do these parties stand for?

From time to time, the parties change their positions or philosophies. Ronald Regan was a Democrat and changed to a Republican. When people accused Ronald Regan of changing political parties, he said, "I did not leave the Democratic Party. They left me." The Democratic Party has, over a period of time, become more liberal in their positions.

Sometimes, there is a third party called an Independent Party where the candidate has views different from the two basic parties.

As you compare these two political parties, just reflect on what Henry Ford, the founder of the Ford Motor Company, said: "If you think the government can run your life better than you can, just look at the American Indians."

The Republican Party

The Republican Party is the conservative party and the party of opportunity. They believe in freedom, opportunity, and individual accountability. The freedom of America is your own ability to make your own decisions about how you live your life with a minimum of restrictive laws. We are a country of laws, but each additional law removes some of our freedom. You have the opportunity to pick your vocation, where to live, and much more. This freedom is not available everywhere in the world. Each person is accountable and responsible for their actions.

- The Republican Party sees the US Constitution as the strong guiding law used by the Supreme Court when our current laws are challenged.
- The main responsibility of the Federal Government is our national security.

- The Republican Party believes in a strong America with a strong military and leadership in the world. The Republican Party is a proponent of democracy in other countries to promote world freedom.
- The Republican Party believes everyone has the freedom and opportunity to improve their lives and that of their family and their children's family.
- The Republican Party believes in a smaller and smarter federal government with more responsibility given to the states that are closer to the people. Fiscal responsibility and a balanced budget are very important.
- As stated in the US Constitution, the government should serve the people to develop an exceptional America that is an example to the world.
- America's biggest problems today are keeping Americans safe and living within our means as a country.

The Democratic Party

The Democratic Party is the liberal party that sees a need for a large government that will control more of a person's rights and liberties—more federal programs of welfare, healthcare, education, and more all controlled at the federal level. They believe in less power for the state government as they believe the federal government can do it better.

- The Democratic Party believes in the redistribution of wealth by taxation and more social programs. The Democratic Party believes it can spend your money better than you can.
- The Democratic Party wants a smaller military and less military spending. They are not interested in America being a leader on the world stage and promoting freedom to other countries.

- The Democratic Party thinks of the US Constitution as an outdated document that needs to be updated to meet the needs of the new America.
- Some of the candidates for the president's office call themselves a progressive candidate. This means they want to have more laws, more taxation, and more social programs. Some even call themselves a socialist candidate, where the government controls most aspects of your life as a result limiting your freedom.
- The Democratic Party is interested in the protection of the environment with an even larger Environmental Protection Agency. They see the largest problem that America faces in the future is global warming.

Who to vote for?

1. Most candidates for political office are very good at producing very convincing speeches and making a lot of promises.
2. What a candidate has done with their life is a good indication of the kind of person they really are.
3. Vote first for the party that matches your beliefs and values and then for your candidate of choice. **This is very important**.

As you listen to the various candidates of each political party, try to evaluate how their views match the descriptions of the parties listed above.

In the 2008 election, a new candidate came on the stage. He talked about bringing "change" to America. We are the best nation in the world by any measure. Why would someone want "change"? Through the use of the internet, he earned the vote and support of the voting youth. The change he brought in was not good, and history will reflect on the result of his failed leadership.

During the 2012 Presidential election President Obama was running for his second term as a Democrat and the Republican challenger was Governor Mitt Romney. It appeared that it was going to be a very close race. When the votes were counted President Obama won by 1%. What was amazing was that only half of the registered Republicans showed up to cast a vote. That is a shame and it is the best definition of "apathy" which is defined by a lack of concern, interest, or enthusiasm. Everyone of age has a right to vote and the responsibility to vote.

Be careful with your vote. Vote to ensure your future, that of your family, and the future of America!

CHAPTER 15

What is Socialism?

During the 2016 presidential primary election, Bernie Sanders, a senator from Vermont decided to run for the office of the president. He is the longest-serving independent in U.S. congressional history. He has spent the majority of his life as a congressman in the House of Representatives and the Senate. He did generate 357 bills, and only 3 became laws. Two were for the postal service in his state of Vermont, and one was for a cost of living adjustment for military service personnel. He was listed as an Independent and ran as a Democrat.

As he started to make a lot of speeches, he drew large crowds of mainly young voters. He received a lot of donations from young voters. What was his magic? It was not magic, but rather it was his message. He was a self-proclaimed socialist. He promised to give everyone in America the right to free healthcare and a free college education. Does this sound too good to be true? He had the young voters following him and voting for him because they wanted something for free.

Nothing in this world is truly free. Everything comes with a price. As one older and wiser person said, "If you get a free college education, you will be paying for it the rest of your life." What he was saying is taxes would have to be increased to provide free education.

When you get out of college and start your first job, you will be paying very high taxes to provide such benefits to everyone else.

The United States of America is a capitalist country. If you start a new company to sell services or goods, then you are expanding the growth of the economy. This is good for everyone. When the government taxes the working people and uses the money to provide benefits for people who do not work or pay taxes, it does not expand the economy. It just moves the money. **Taxation does not grow the economy!**

Bernie Sanders is a good speaker with a lot of passion, and the young voters believe that socialism will work. The story below is an example of how a professor showed his class the truth about socialism.

How socialism works (See Note 15-1)

An economics professor at a college in Lubbock, Texas made a statement that he had never failed a single student before but had recently failed an entire class. That class had insisted Obama's socialism worked and that no one would be poor and no one would be rich—a great equalizer.

The professor then said, "OK, we will have an experiment in this class on Obama's plan." All grades will be averaged, and everyone will receive the same grade. So no one will fail, and no one will receive an A. He substituted grades for dollars—something closer to home and more readily understood by all.

After the first test, the grades were averaged, and everyone got a B. The students who studied hard were upset, and the students who studied less were happy. As the second test rolled around, the students who studied less had studied even lesser, and the ones who studied hard decided they wanted a free ride too so they studied less.

The second test average was a D! No one was happy. When the third test rolled around, the average was an F.

As the tests proceeded, the scores never increased as bickering, blame, and name-calling all resulted in hard feelings and no one would study for the benefit of anyone else.

To their great surprise, ALL FAILED. The professor told them socialism would also ultimately fail because when the reward is great, the effort to succeed is great, but when government takes all the reward away, no one will try or want to succeed. It could not be any simpler than that. These are possibly the five best sentences you'll ever read, and all are applicable to this experiment:

1. **You cannot legislate the poor into prosperity by legislating the wealthy out of prosperity.**
2. **What one person receives without working for, another person must work for without receiving.**
3. **The government cannot give to anybody anything that the government does not first take from somebody else.**
4. **You cannot multiply wealth by dividing it!**
5. **When half of the people get the idea that they do not have to work because the other half is going to take care of them, and when the other half gets the idea that it does no good to work because somebody else is going to get what they work for, that is the beginning of the end of any nation.**

In 2015, it was stated that of the fifty states in this country, ten states had more people on welfare than people working. When there are more people riding in the wagon than pulling the wagon, we have a real problem.

Adding to the problem is that people have little incentive to get off welfare and get a job because they make more money on welfare than taking an entry-level job.

The national debt is over twenty trillion dollars, and that is about sixty thousand dollars of debt for each man, woman, and child in America. This must be addressed, and that is one of the key points in the 2016 presidential election.

What is progressive government?

When you listen to the news, you will hear some Democrats state they are progressives. Even President Obama says he is a progressive president. Hilary Clinton says she is a progressive candidate. What are they trying to say?

What does the Webster Dictionary say about the word *progressive*?

1. Happening or developing gradually or in stages
2. Proceeding step by step
3. Continuing, continuous, increasing, growing
4. Developing, ongoing, accelerating, escalating, gradual, cumulative
5. Forward thinking, modern, liberal, advanced, enlightened
6. Enterprising, innovative, pioneering, dynamic, bold
7. Reforming, reformist, radical, go-ahead, reactionary

When you hear talk about the right and left views on politics, the conservatives are on the right and the liberals are on the left. The Republican Party is the conservative party, and the Democrats are the liberal party.

Who is left of the Democrats? It is the progressives. Their views are of larger federal government and less freedom for individuals. They sell their views as more pioneering, bold, radical, growing, and proceeding step by step, but in reality, they are taking away your opportunity and freedom until one day, this great country of United States of America, is no longer the greatest country in the world.

What is left of the progressives? It is the socialists.

America was founded on some very import ideas. It is not patterned after the countries in Europe or Asia. It was founded on IDEAS. America was founded on ideas of freedom and opportunity for all and the idea that people had the right to choose their own path and do whatever they wanted to do unless they violated someone else's rights.

God has blessed America in so many ways. With 5 percent of the world's population, America has 50 percent of the world's wealth. That is just one measure. The greatest measure is that every family wants their children to have a better life than their parents. In America, this is the true value of our success. Now this family growth to have a better life is in jeopardy of being lost due to the twenty-trillion-dollar debt this generation has incurred. This will have to be paid by someone! As interest rates start to increase, the interest we pay will increase substantially.

Thomas Jefferson was the third president of our great country. He believed each generation should pay for their own debts. Will our children have to pay for our debt of twenty trillion dollars?

Thomas Jefferson was considered one of the wisest men to become president. This is one of his famous quotations:

> **"A wise and frugal government, which shall restrain men from injuring one another, shall leave them otherwise free to regulate their own pursuits of industry and improvement, and shall not take from the mouth of labor the bread it has earned."**

As a country develops, it has a tendency to become more and more socialistic. The countries of Europe have moved to become more socialistic, and we in America are also heading in that direction.

It has been said, "Give a man a loaf of bread and you feed him for a day. But give a man a job and you feed him for a lifetime."

We need to get America working again—*everybody* working!

CHAPTER 16

Do You Have the "Want To"?

While working for a certain food service company, I was responsible for a number of departments. One of which was training and development.

I sent the training manager to a seminar on the latest training tools that were being implemented by the industry. When the training manager returned to work, she asked me the following question: "What is the most important quality one should seek when hiring a new employee?"

I listed qualities such as knowledge, experience, a good work record, good personal references, and the like. She said at the seminar, it was stated the most important quality to look for in a new hire is the "want to." Without the "want to," everything else really does not matter. The "want to" is simply a positive attitude with self-motivation.

This reminds me of a situation I experienced while working for Walt Disney World. I was hiring a new department secretary, and she had been screened by the personnel department. She had excellent typing and shorthand skills. After an interview, she was offered the position and accepted.

She had some very interesting ideas about good work habits. She would come in late and then leave early to make it up. She would make a lot of personal calls from the office. This was before cell phones. She had a yellow princess phone installed in her apartment, and she had to call the phone company right away because they used a gray phone cord on the yellow phone. This was an emergency in her mind. Her work was of second importance. She did not have the "want to," even though she had exceptional skills.

She kept coming to me and telling me this was not the right job for her. I kept encouraging her to keep trying. After the third time she approached me about her concern that it was not the right job, I agreed and told her she was free to leave. She went back to the personnel department in tears and said she did not know what happened. They reassigned her to another area.

One company I worked for stated in their training program that there were only three reasons why people will not do what you want them to do. They are as follows:

1. They don't know what is expected.
2. They can't do the job.
3. They have a bad attitude.

If they don't know what is expected, it is a training solution. If they can't do the job, it is a reassignment solution if possible. If they have a bad attitude, they need to fix the attitude or leave.

This works great for evaluating employees but does not work with family members. But it might help one find the root of the problem.

The "want to" is attitude—just that simple.

The root of the problem

In the restaurant business, there are a lot of moving parts. A restaurant is manufacturing a product and also selling the items and providing a service to the customer or the guest. This complicates the management as it is really a team effort and all members of the team must work in coordination with others on the team.

The goal is to serve hot food hot and cold food cold with good, sincere hospitality. Sounds easy. Training and attitude are the keys. When we find cold food served at room temperature and hot food served cold, there is a problem with the execution of the team. But where is the problem?

Providing the restaurant has a lot of operational problems, there is normally a central reason for the problem. The reason is normally the manager of the restaurant. They are normally the root of the problem. They are not providing the leadership to motivate the employees to strive for excellence.

Once you find the root of the problem or problems, it is easy to solve the problem and implement the solution.

CHAPTER 17

The Atheist College Professor

In your life, you will meet a number of nonbelievers. Most have a very personal reason why they are nonbelievers. When this happens, you should just pray for the person, and if enough people pray for them, hopefully someday they too will see the light.

Many of the teachers in high schools and universities are very liberal in their thinking, and it is not only with their personal beliefs, but also in their teachings.

This is a story of one such liberal teacher who was also a nonbeliever.

On the first day of class, a college professor asked for a volunteer student who believed in God to come to the front of the class to answer some questions about their personal beliefs. One young man stepped forward and said he would answer the professor's questions if he could.

The professor first thanked the student for volunteering and then asked if he believed in God. The student stated a definite yes. Next, the professor asked if God created man and allowed him to sin if he wanted. Again, the student said yes. Next, the professor asked if God created everything. The student again stated yes. Then the professor asked if God created evil. The student was perplexed and did not answer. Then the professor stated that if God created everything, then He must have created evil. The student did not respond as he was not sure of the answer.

A student from the back of the room asked the professor, "Did God create light?" The professor stated that "If God created everything, He must have created light." Then the student from the back of the room asked the question, "Did God create dark?" Again, the professor stated, "If God created everything, He must have created dark."

The student from the back of the room continued, "God did not create dark. Dark is a name we give a situation where there is an absence of all light."

The professor started to think to himself that it was going to be a good semester as he enjoyed such exchanges with students.

The student from the back of the room continued, "Did God create heat?" Again, the professor stated, "If God created everything, God must have created heat."

The student from the back of the room asked, "Did God create cold?"

The professor stated, "If God created everything, He must have created cold."

The student from the back of the room stated, "God did not create cold. Cold is just a name we give the situation where there is no heat and it is at absolute zero, which is minus 273.15 degrees Celsius.

The student continued, "God did not create evil as evil is the absence of God with his love, mercy, and grace. It is the same situation as cold or dark. Evil is what we experience when there is the absence of God, His Word, and His Blessings. It is the work of Satan."

Who was that student with his profound logic? Story says it might have been Albert Einstein.

"The fool says in his heart,
'There is no God.'"
(Psalms 14:1)

———•••———

"Whoever acknowledges me before others,
I will also acknowledge before my Father in heaven.
But whoever disowns me before others,
I will disown before my Father in
heaven" (Matthew 10:32–33).

CHAPTER 18

Finance and Investing

It has been said that money is the root of all evil. It is not that money is the root of all evil, but rather it is the **love** of money that is the root of all evil. Money will not solve all your problems. There are a lot of successful people who are very good at making money, but they are not happy or content with their lives.

(See note 18-1)

Publicly operated lotteries exist in more than one hundred countries. In recent years, lottery ticket sales totaled more than 85 billion dollars in just the United States and Canada. That's only part of the total sales worldwide. The lure of huge jackpots has created a mindset among many that all of life's problems would be solved "if I won the lottery."

There is nothing wrong with wealth itself, but it has the power to deceive us into thinking money is the answer to all our needs.

The psalmist, expressing a different point of view, wrote:

> *"I have rejoiced in your laws as in riches.*
> *as one rejoices in great riches.*
> *I will delight in your decrees;*
> *And not forget your word."*
> (Psalms 119:14, 16 NLT)

This concept of spiritual treasure is focused on obedience to God and walking *"in the path of His commands."* (Psalms 119:35)

What if we were more excited about following the Lord's Word than about winning a jackpot worth millions? With the psalmist we might pray. "Incline my heart to your testimonies, and not to covetousness. Turn away my eyes from looking at worthless things, and revive me in Your way." (Psalms 119:36-37)

The riches of obedience—true riches—belong to all who walk with the Lord.

(See note 18-2)

Read God's Word in the Bible and all the wisdom contained therein. Start with the thirty-one chapters of Proverbs, and read one each day. Do this at least twice a year, and you will be amazed at how this will change your life. It is worth more than winning the lottery.

The quality of our children's education is not what it once was and not what it should be to properly prepare them for today's life. Our children are not getting the basics of a good, balanced education. Particularly, they are not getting the basics of sound personal finance. What is missing? **Just about everything.**

First, we should put God's Word back in our schools. In addition to God's Word in the Bible, we should also include subjects such as these to properly prepare our children for their future:

1. Budgeting
2. Financing a home
3. Managing credit cards
4. Balancing a checkbook
5. How to set up a plan for savings
6. How to buy a car
7. How to buy a house
8. Managing interest expenses
9. How to invest in your future

When in college, I had an outstanding professor in the area of personal finance. He had a simple plan to make and grow money, but it takes discipline. He said when one graduates and takes a job, they will see a sharp increase in their income. Most Americans have a cost of living that is 110 percent of their take-home pay; therefore, they are always in debt and paying interest. The professor's plan was as follows: When you graduate, save and invest 10 percent of your income each and every year. By the time one retires, they should have one million dollars in investments. It is not easy and it takes a lot of discipline, but it will work.

In high school, I was on the track team but far from being a track star. I liked the short races where I could go as fast as I could for a short distance. I would run the 100-yard dash, the 220-yard dash, the 120-yard low hurdles and was on the 440-yard 4-man relay team.

In business and in investing, I would approach that task at hand the same way. I was looking for very fast results. I should have used a longer time period to expect results from my investment. Someone said to me, "Life is not a sprint but rather a long-distance race, and one should make decisions for the long-term and not the short-term."

Here are a few things to remember when making large purchases:

1. If you buy something on credit, it should be something that normally appreciates in value, such as a home. The best investment reason to own your own home is because of inflation. Normally, inflation is about 2 percent per year. As you own your own home, its value will increase as

long as you continue to keep its appearance or improve its condition. It can be your best investment as long as you do not buy a home that is more than you can afford.

2. When you buy a home, make sure you shop the interest rates. You are buying the home, but you are also buying the cost of using the money you are borrowing. That is the rate of interest. Also compare the closing costs from one loan to another. Ask a lot of questions if you are not sure.

3. You should save your money and buy with cash for those things that will depreciate in value, such as a car. I know this is not easy because it is our nature to want it NOW!

4. When buying large purchases, such as a car or a home, try to buy below the market. Then you can sell at the market and make a profit.

5. If you sell one home to buy another, put your equity in the new home. Your goal is to have your home paid off before retirement.

6. You can save big with this idea. People buy lots of furniture on credit and then get a divorce and have to liquidate at a lower price. You can buy very good quality used furniture on places like Craigslist, but be selective and be careful.

7. **If you use credit cards, make sure you pay them off each month so you will have no interest expense.** Credit card interest is very high, and that is why one should pay off the balance each month. Credit cards can get away from you if you are not careful. I recommend using a credit card that offers some type of reward like "cash back." I also recommend using only **one** credit card as it is easier to control if you only have one. Some people have ten or fifteen cards, and that is much more difficult to manage.

Investments

Good investment advisers are hard to find. They want to make a profit at your expense. There is a saying that nothing will make you broke faster than a stockbroker. Stockbrokers are sales people. Many times, they are selling what the firm wants them to sell and not what is your best investment. Proceed with caution. **Invest your time before you invest your money. Be patient in your expectation of results.**

Save and invest for the future. Land and homes you can rent are normally good investments. With land, you must select one that will have a good opportunity for appreciation because you will have taxes to pay each year. With a rental home, make sure you can take time to properly manage the property or get a professional to manage it for you. Rental property is a great investment as the cash coming in pays the principle and interest on your investment.

Save for the future and the unexpected. You should have a reserve for emergencies equal to six months' take-home salary. It is easy to want something you cannot afford, so heed this warning. Proceed with caution. **Dealing with money takes discipline.**

Remember, your best advisor is God and His Word in the Bible.

"What good is it for someone to gain the whole world, yet forfeit their soul?" (Mark 8:36).

◆

"But seek first his kingdom and his righteousness, and all these things will be given to you as well" (Matthew 6:33).

◆

"And my God will meet all your needs according to the riches of his glory in Christ Jesus" (Philippians 4:19).

◆

"Keep your lives free from the love of money and be content with what you have, because God has said, 'Never will I leave you; never will I forsake you.'" (Hebrew 13:5)

CHAPTER 19

Great Summer Jobs
and Learning to Live Longer

During my college days, I wanted to work in different summer jobs. I felt the experience would enrich me with job-related knowledge and enhance my job-seeking resume. I sought adventure and did not want to work in the same job each year. I could also earn money to help with my education.

When we are young, we look out to the future and think we are invincible. We think we will live forever. Sometimes, we take chances we should not take. These are the everyday choices that can turn out very bad if one does not take careful consideration of what might happen. What might be the consequences of our actions?

One summer, I worked in a pizza takeout place owned by the person who gave me my first job. That was not my idea of an exciting job.

Just after high school, I had one very good friend who was an exceptional artist. We talked about working at Yosemite National Park during the summer of 1964. We both wanted to buy motorcycles so we could ride around Yosemite. To say the least, my parents did not want me to get a motorcycle. The Beach Boys had a song that made the Honda 50 very popular at the time, and we both wanted a Honda 90. After a time, my parents said OK, but they were not happy with my decision. **Again, I was listening to my friend to make my decisions and not my parents.**

I had the Honda 90 for three months and got into three accidents. I got rid of it before it got rid of me. My parents were right about how dangerous motorcycles can be. I goofed—enough said!!

I still liked the idea of working at Yosemite and pursued employment there. It was very competitive as a lot of college students wanted to work there. I was turned down the first time I applied, but I did not stop there.

When I was nineteen years old, after my freshman year at Glendale College, I successfully got a summer job at Yosemite National Park. That was a real eye opener for me as it was the first time I was away from home the entire summer. I met a friend, Tom, who was a graduate from the City College of San Francisco's Hotel And Restaurant Department. When I first met him, I was working in the kitchen of the main restaurant in Camp Curry. I was hired to be a "chef's helper," and when I arrived at Yosemite, they made me a vegetable prep cook. At that time, I thought it was a downgrade. After arriving at that kitchen, I learned the chef's helper was really a dishwasher. It is funny how things turn out.

I was the type of person employers wanted because I followed directions to the tee. When I met Tom, he walked up to me and said, "You are doing that all wrong!" I told him to tell Chef Paul because that was how he instructed me to do the work. It was a rough start, but we became good friends and shared an apartment my first semester when I attended the City College of San Francisco.

It was a great summer, and I learned a lot. Yosemite is one of the true national treasures of this country as it has real beauty everywhere. There is El Capitan at 3,000 feet above the valley floor and Bridal Veil Waterfall which is 620 feet above the valley floor. This waterfall got its name because when the wind hit the water it looks like a bridal veil.

The Fire Falls were presented every evening. A large bonfire was built on the cliff above the valley floor. The fire would burn down until it was a pile of very large red hot embers. Shortly after sunset, the burning embers would be pushed off the rim of the cliff with a large rake. This would create the impression of a burning waterfall in the night sky.

Every morning, as the guests would come to the Camp Curry cafeteria for breakfast, they would talk about the beauty of the Fire Falls. Some thought it was made by lights in the back of a waterfall. Others said they would float burning logs over a waterfall. It was fun to hear all the experts on how they tried to explain the Fire Falls. Later, the Fire Falls were eliminated because it was considered to take away from the real beauty of the Yosemite Valley.

Hiking alone

There was another large granite formation called Half Dome. It was over 4,700 feet above the valley floor. I heard one could hike up to the top of Half Dome. On one of my days off, I decided to make that hike on my own. It is not really safe to hike alone, and I should have gone with someone. But I am a bit of a loner and a bit independent, so off I went one morning.

The round trip hike was eighteen-miles and one should properly prepare for such a hike, but off I went with no water, food, or anything. When I reached the massive granite rock, I first came to Quarter Dome, a smaller rock. Behind it was the massive granite Half Dome. When I reached the top of Quarter Dome, I saw the huge granite mountain ahead of me. Up the side of the granite were steel cables and pipes drilled into the granite to help the hikers reach the summit. There were wooden boards attached to the steel pipes where one could stop and catch their breath. It was much steeper than I had imagined, but off I went.

I have a fear of heights called "acrophobia" and was really scared. But I had come that far, and there was no turning back. I did reach the top and felt great about that, as it was at a total elevation of 8,694 feet. I did not get close to the edge as one side had a straight drop of 4,737 feet to the valley floor.

When it was time to start back, I came to the top of the steel cable leading the way down. It was so steep that I could not see the bottom half of the cable ladder as it was not visible. It looked like it was going straight down. What should I do? Taking one small section of this ladder, I ventured down. Going down was much harder than coming up because you were looking straight down. To make things worse, people were coming up at the same time I was going down.

When I got to the bottom of the cable ladder, I was very thirsty. I had hiked about ten miles in the heat of the day with no water. That was not smart. The mountain was so high I was above the rivers formed by runoff from the melting snow. As I continued my return hike, I finally reached a river of cool water and drank and drank and drank. When I reached the floor of the valley, I was so tired I could barely walk. Although I was not hungry, I did make it to the Camp Curry cafeteria where I ate some ice-cold watermelon.

When we are in the ages of young adulthood, we have "no fear." Risk assessment is a tool that develops at the ages twenty-two to twenty-four. Some people never get risk assessment. **Risk assessment is just seeing the danger that exists before one starts to venture into a situation.**

When one is in their teens, they are influenced a lot by their friends, the newest fad, and the newest drug because they want to be part of the "in" crowd. They think they are invincible and will live forever. They drive too fast and sometimes test the bounds of reality.

Every sport has certain rules we should always obey. With hiking, one should never hike alone. One should take enough food and water for a longer period of time than the expected hike. One should tell someone where they are going and when they expect to return. This is all common sense. When you have no fear, you do not have or use your common sense. **It has been said if common sense was really common, more people would have it.**

There are many stories of people who hiked alone and ran into some real problems. I remember a story about a very accomplished mountain climber and outdoorsman who decided to go for a desert hike alone.

When he was climbing on some very large boulders, one of the boulders slipped and crushed his hand and forearm between that boulder and another one. He was trapped, and no one knew he was there. It was hot, and he just had one canteen of water. He was worried about getting dehydrated. After his water was gone, he had to save his urine in his canteen to drink so he would not get dehydrated. He did not tell anyone where he was going, except that he was going for a hike. After five days, he decided the only way to get out alive was to cut his arm off below the elbow. He could not cut through the bone, so he had to break his arm so he could cut himself free. To find all the details, look on the web for the book *Between a Rock and a Hard Place* and the movie *127 Hours*.

My message here is that life is fragile, and we should avoid dangerous situations. Remember your priorities in life.

1. Is this something God approves of?
2. Is this something my parents approve of?

Here are a few more real life stories that took place in my life. As you read them, you will see I did not use good judgment. Now I know God was watching over me.

Scuba diving

I have another example I would like to share. While in high school, I was interested in scuba diving. I liked watching the TV program called *Sea Hunt* about adventures in scuba diving. I took a class at a small dive shop to get certified and bought a used tank and regulator and all the other gear one needed. I took a second dive class at Glendale College and received a second certification. The four rules of scuba diving are:

1. Never dive alone.
2. Always dive with a partner.
3. Never hold your breath.
4. Always continue to breathe.

One day, I decided to go scuba diving, and I did have a partner. We decided to go to the cliffs at Pacific Palisades in Southern California. At that time, the waters in that area were rich in sea life, and sometimes, we could find abalone, a beautiful shellfish off the California Coast. The meat of the abalone is considered a delicacy.

I spotted a commercial fishing boat that was floating off the shore and was just drifting. I wanted to go and check it out and my partner didn't want to join me, so I ventured out on my own to see what the problem was. The fishing boat had gotten its fishing net caught on the bottom of the boat close to the propeller, and the boat was not moving. They did not want to tangle the net in the propeller.

I surfaced close to the boat. They asked me to pull the net out of the area where it was being held. I went under the boat and pulled the net out so they could pull it into the boat. They were very appreciative and wanted to give me some fish. I declined because I did not want to drag dead fish back to shore. I was concerned about sharks. I was not very smart as lots of bad things could have happened if they had started up the engine while I was under the boat. At that time in my life, I did not see the danger.

Another time, I was diving off Catalina Island, which is about twenty-six miles off the California coast. We would normally dive in thirty to thirty-five feet of water. At that depth, there was a lot of sea life in the kelp beds. The island and has spiny lobsters, moray eels and very large gold colored fish called Garibaldi. I was diving off a dive boat and did have a partner. We got separated, and I started heading into deeper water. The floor of the ocean dropped off very fast, and before I knew it, I was on the bottom at one hundred feet. That was not a safe thing to do because if I had a problem of any kind, I would be alone. I went back and found my dive partner. Again, I did not see the danger.

Sailing to Catalina Island

When I was twenty-four and working at Disneyland, I decided to join a sailing club at Balboa Island in Southern California near

Newport Beach. As a member, I could use the sailboats one day a month for my membership dues. The sailboats were a Cal 27, and they were only twenty-seven feet long. I would sail them around Balboa Island and sometimes venture into the Pacific Ocean.

Two friends who also worked at Disneyland expressed an interest in going sailing someday. I suggested a trip to Catalina Island. As the song goes, it is located twenty-six miles off the coast of California. At best, the boats would sail only five knots per hour, which is slightly faster than five miles per hour. So with good wind, it would take, at best, six hours to sail each way. We decided to sail over one day and return the next day. We were sailing out of Newport Beach, so it was slightly farther than twenty-six miles.

Our boat was equipped with a compass, a chart of the California Coast, a chart of Catalina Island, and life jackets. We did not have any type of marine radio or any other way to communicate if we ran into problems. The island is twenty-two-miles long and eight-miles wide at the widest point. We were headed to Avalon, the only town on the island, and it is located on the South end of the island.

We left at about ten in the morning. The wind was good, and its direction was good for a straight run to Avalon. The visibility was listed by the weather station at thirteen miles, so our rough calculation was we would lose sight of the main land and then we would see the island. We sailed for a few hours, making good time, and could no longer see the coast. As we continued toward the island, my crew of nonsailors were getting concerned that they could not see the island. On a clear day, one can see Catalina Island from the California Coast.

As we continued to sail several more hours, my crew was ready to head back to the coast. We knew we could not miss the coast. About an hour later, and many checks of the chart, the town of Avalon came into view. To say the least, there was a more relaxed feeling on the boat. My crew thought we were going to miss the island altogether. We could not see the island as there was a light haze surrounding it.

We visited Avalon, spent the night on the boat, and returned the following day without incident. The return trip was much less stressful as we knew we could not miss the California Coast.

We should have made arrangements to take a portable marine radio with us. This was in 1970, and there were no cell phones. We should have made better safety arrangements in case of mechanical difficulties, sickness, injuries, or sinking. We should have worn the life jackets, but we did not. We should have brought an emergency supply of food and water in case our trip had lasted longer than two days.

We did not see the possible danger in what we were doing. Again, my life has been blessed by God in so many ways.

Tragic fishing story

On February 28, 2009, two NFL players, one trainer, and a friend ventured out into the Gulf of Mexico for a day of fishing. At the end of the day, they were trying to dislodge the anchor, and it flipped their boat. Three of the crew died and only one survived after forty-three hours of clinging to the capsized boat.

You can read about the entire unfortunate story in the book *Not Without Hope* by Nick Schuyler, the only survivor of the fishing trip. They were in a twenty-one-foot boat that was considered small to be thirty-one miles off the coast, and the weather was changing and causing five to seven foot waves. In addition, they had been drinking most of the day.

Another tragic story

I wanted to tell you one additional sad story where young adults did not use good common sense. This story takes place at the beautiful Bridal Veil Falls in Yosemite National Park. Just a few years ago, I heard on the news that some college students were swimming at the top of the falls. One of the girls started to get too close to the edge and started yelling for help. Her boyfriend came to the rescue, but when he reached her, they could not fight the current of the river. They were both swept over the edge and killed. This is so sad because it could have been avoided. They had no fear. They did not have a risk assessment and did not see the danger. They did not consider the consequences of their actions.

On the lighter side

I want to share an additional story about Yosemite and Camp Curry. Camp Curry was not a hotel or even a motel. It was a camp of tents with wooden floors, canvas roofs, and canvas sides. Some of the college students worked at the check-in desk and assisted new visitors to be assigned to their tents. Two older ladies were checking in at the center and saw a squirrel. Not being familiar with squirrels, she asked the clerk what it was. He replied, "Ladies, this is the only place in the United States that has bushy tailed rats." The ladies decided to leave the park immediately, and the clerk found his summer employment cut short due to his sense of humor.

I spent two summers at Yosemite National Park and enjoyed it very much. The first summer, I worked in the main kitchen at the Camp Curry complex, serving a number of restaurants.

The second summer, I worked at the Ahwanee Hotel that is a AAA Four Diamond Hotel. I worked in the cold kitchen, making box lunches, salads, and salad dressings including the mayonnaise that we made in ten-gallon batches. The Ahwanee Hotel is operated with the American meal plan, so three meals per day are included in the price of the room. It is a beautiful hotel that was built in 1927.

Another great summer job

While going to the City College of San Francisco, I learned of a very unusual summer job with Pan American Airways. Each summer, Pan American Airways would visit the food service management program and select six students to work for the summer as stewards on flights out of San Francisco.

That sounded like the perfect job. It was the summer of 1966, and I was twenty-one years old. I talked to some of the students who worked for Pan American during the summer of 1965, and they said it was a great summer job. Pan American Airways was considered the flagship of America. They were considered the best of the best. Menus in the first class section included prime rib, steaks, seafood, and a selection of fine wines.

The students who were in the program the year before said it was a great opportunity. After two weeks of extensive training on safety and airline operation at the Stewardess Training Center in Miami, they took a training flight from San Francisco to Hawaii. The next flight was to any location of their choice in the Pacific area. After that, they had to bid for flights with the union rules. Since the students had the lowest seniority, they mainly flew from San Francisco to Hawaii and return. Not bad for a summer job. (Side note: At that time, flight attendants were called stewards and stewardesses.)

I applied for the program and was selected as one of the six participants. We had to get our uniforms and a lot of shots. About two weeks before the program started, we were scheduled to leave for Miami. They called the group in to tell us the program had to be eliminated. To say the least, we were very disappointed.

One of the senior flight stewards wanted his son to be in the program. Because he did not have the same type of training, the company said he could not be in the program, so the senior flight steward said if his son could not be in the program, he would file a grievance with the union. The company made the decision that it would cancel the program rather than fight the grievance. The company was really great because they understood we had only two weeks to find a new summer job and said if we wanted to work on projects for the company, they would give us summer jobs with the possibility of some travel. Sometimes, a disappointment can work out to be really great.

It is said when God closes one door, he opens another. If one is so focused on the closed door and the disappointment, they might not see the open door and what it might offer. I took their job offer as did five of the six in the program.

We worked at the San Francisco Airport for about one week, just helping out where needed, mostly in the office. The United Airlines went on strike right at the start of the summer travel time. In those days, only two US airlines flew to Hawaii, and that was United and Pan American. Since United was on strike, Pan American was hit with a lot of reservations that overloaded the reservation system.

To assist with the situation, we were asked to go to the main reservation office in downtown San Francisco. Some of the flights were overbooked by as much as one hundred passengers, and they had to be notified about the change to different flights and different flight times. As we called some of the passengers, they thought we were one of their neighbors playing a joke on them. It took some convincing before they believed it was Pan American. We worked most of the summer at the reservation office.

Since United was on strike, Pan American flights were all at 100 percent capacity between San Francisco and Hawaii. There was not much hope to fly standby to Hawaii. One of the members of our group said, "Why not fly us standby to Tokyo and then back to Hawaii since those flights are not at capacity?" So two of the group left the next day to work in Hawaii for two weeks via Japan.

I was the last one to go and, therefore, I traveled alone. I first flew to Tokyo and stayed for three days before I traveled to Hawaii. They put me up in the same hotels that were used for the flight crews, and in Hawaii, it was right on Waikiki Beach. I had requested to work in the commissary operations because of my interest in food service. I got to know the commissary manager, and he showed me plans of the expansion of the facilities because they were planning to provide the food service for a very large plane that would hold up to five hundred passengers. It was the Boeing 747.

I asked the commissary manager if he needed additional help during the busy summer travel time, and he said he did. I told him if he had a job open, I would like to apply for it, doing whatever they needed. He said if I could get to Hawaii, I had a job as a port steward, and I could fly back at no charge if I traveled standby. As a port steward, I would be loading the planes with food.

The summer of 1967, I worked in Hawaii. On the way over to Hawaii, I met two guys who were going to be working at the airport in the passenger check-in area. One was from University of Chicago, and the other was from Brown University. We shared a small studio apartment one block from Waikiki Beach. I mainly worked the three to eleven shift, so I had time to enjoy the beach in the morning. I also took a hike to the top of Diamond Head and saw the gun bunker from World War II at the top of the mountain. It was a great summer. Again, my life has been blessed by God.

The summer of 1967 was after my first semester at Cornell University. Disney was recruiting for summer jobs at Disneyland, and they previewed the plans Walt had for the Epcot Center located in Central Florida. I interviewed with Disney and told them I was interested in the next year since I had a summer job for 1967.

In the summer of 1968, I worked at Disneyland as a summer assistant supervisor. I worked six days a week at Tomorrow Terrace and was responsible for the operation of the night shift. That was about four in the afternoon until the job was done normally until one in the morning.

During my performance review, halfway through the summer, my supervisor asked the question, "How does your education compare with the duties on your job here?" I replied that at school, most of the class subjects were law, economics, restaurant design, and selection of food service equipment, hotel maintenance, food preparation, and sanitation. Most of my summer work was working with the staff—employee relations and proper staffing levels. My supervisor said Disney was really not in the restaurant business but rather in the **people business**.

That was a red flag that **should** have made me stop and think. Was this the best career for me? Not that Disney was a bad company. It was not. It showed a lot of future potential. But I was not a people person, and food operations is all about people. I was serving people, motivating people, disciplining people, counseling people, and evaluating people. It takes a certain type of person to do this job and love it. **It was not one of my gifts and not a strong trait of mine**.

Some people just fit in their chosen profession, and some people just don't fit. Some people just love their work, but the majority say the workers dislike the time they spend working. It is said that if you love your job, you never work a day in your life. **It is a big decision**. Get it right, and it will pay you dividends your entire life. This is a very important decision as it will affect your **happiness and, to a large degree, your success.**

Like many people, I have reflected on my life and the choices I have made and wondered, "What if I could live my life over?" What would I do the same, and what would I do differently?

I am pleased with some of the choices I made, but now, I know there is a better way. It is simply not possible to live my life again, so why spend time discussing the idea? We cannot drive our cars looking in the rearview mirror.

Many young people look at life the same way. They have no fear and think their life will go on forever. They don't fully understand how the choices they make will affect their entire life. When one is young, life looks like it will last forever, but as one gets older, life looks much shorter. Even looking back over one's life it seems like a movie that went by in a flash. The years go by so much faster as one gets older.

We should enjoy the day and all it has to offer. Make the most of everyday.

It is so wisely stated:

> **"We cannot change the past.**
> **We do not know the future.**
> **Live each day to the fullest as**
> **it certainly is a gift.**
> **That is why we call it,**
> **'the Present.'"**

Life is funny.

I had the opportunity to work in both Hawaii and Disneyland. When I was working in Hawaii and asked people where they would go for the perfect vacation, they would say "Disneyland." When I worked at Disneyland, I asked the same question, and people would say, "Hawaii." The grass in always greener someplace else.

CHAPTER 20

Working for Walt
Disney Productions

I worked for Disneyland after graduating from Cornell University in June of 1969, in addition to my summer internship during the summer of 1968. One of my main motivations was to be part of the opening of Walt Disney World in Florida in October 1971.

While I was at the City College of San Francisco, I remember hearing the news that Walt Disney had passed away. Walt was the dreamer, and his brother Roy Disney was the one who worked with the banks to provide financing for Walt's dreams.

When a person works under the shadow of the founder of the company, a lot of people do what they do because they think it is what Walt would have done. Many do not consider the objective analysis side of the business but more the subjective side of the business philosophies.

When Walt built Disneyland, he had stretched the financial resources of the company. Therefore, he decided to lease out the operation of the restaurants and food stands to outside companies. During the first ten years, there were many complaints about the quality of the food and the high prices. The operators had a captive audience and took advantage of that position to charge high prices for the food. Walt wanted people to remember the beautiful main street, the Cinderella castle, and the attractions, not the high prices for food. So when the leases were up, Walt took over the operation of the food service and hired professionals to operate the food services under the Disney philosophy.

When Walt started his career in Missouri, he was an animator. His first character was Oswald the Lucky Rabbit in 1927, and this was during the era of silent films. He developed this character, and through a licensing agreement gone bad, he lost his right to that character. This was before Mickey Mouse was developed.

After that experience, Walt said he would never let that happen again, but rather he would protect his work for the future. Today, the Disney library of films is a gold mine for the company. Many popular movies are released on a cycle of every seven years. Parents want their children to enjoy the films they enjoyed as children.

This is how some of the "Disney philosophies" were developed into a sound business plan.

When Disney was getting ready to purchase land for Walt Disney World in Florida, they wanted to keep it a secret because if people knew what they were doing, the price of the land would sky rocket. One of the rumors was that the new Disney Park would be located in the Miami area, so to help promote this rumor, Disney sent some people to start to get pricing on land in the Miami area. This took the eyes off the central Florida area. In the central Florida area, Disney was able to lock in a very large amount of land from a number of different sellers by buying options that locked in the purchase and the price. If the word got out, they would be protected on the price.

After securing over twenty thousand acres of land, they received another option for five thousand more acres. This went back to the Disney headquarters in California for discussion. One person said they had plenty of land for all future plans. Walt said, "What would we do if we could get another five thousand acres next to Disneyland in Southern California? Buy it! The Disney property in Florida has over twenty-seven thousand acres of land.

I left the Disney Organization in 1984 after fifteen years working at Disneyland as part of the opening team for Walt Disney World and Tokyo Disneyland.

When I left Disney, the cost of admission for a one-day ticket was about eighteen dollars, and now, due to inflation, it is over a hundred dollars depending on the time of year. The Disney properties have been called the "happiest place on earth." But there is a happier place, and that is the kingdom of God in Heaven. The price of admission is FREE—paid in full by Jesus dying on the cross for our sins. Just ask Him for the gift of Salvation.

CHAPTER 21

The Fire

While attending the City College of San Francisco, it was a requirement to work in the college food service to gain practical knowledge of all areas of food service.

I started in January of 1965 at the age of twenty, and during my first semester, I worked in the short-order snack bar, rotating through all the jobs from prep to cashier. The class ran from eight in the morning till one in the afternoon, five days a week, and I received six credit hours for the thirty hours that I worked. After one, I had to attend class for the additional ten credit hours for the semester.

I was living with a friend who had interested me in the food service program. We shared a small apartment in Sausalito, a small bayside town with a lot of character located just north of the Golden Gate Bridge. It was a long drive to the college, but it worked out alright.

In the fall of 1965, I had to take the next class that would start at seven in the morning till twelve noon, five days a week. I had worked the summer at Yosemite National Park, and when I returned to San Francisco, I decided to just rent a room that was close to the college due to the seven o'clock starting time for the class.

There was a listing on the college bulletin board for a room to rent, and I went to check the place out. It was a nice clean house on one of the hills with a beautiful view of the valley. It was very close to the college, so I could make my morning class without the long commute.

The house had three bedrooms, a living room, dining room, and kitchen all on the upper level. The ground level consisted of a small apartment and the garage. My room was on the upper level, just over the garage.

A nice lady owned the home and also lived there. She rented the master bedroom to a retired Navy man. The one-bedroom apartment on the ground floor was also for rent, and she wanted one hundred and ten dollars per month. I paid fifty-five dollars a month for my room and kitchen privileges, and I shared a bathroom with the owner of the home.

This seemed like a perfect situation for me. Monday through Friday, I would go to school and study. On the weekends, I would go to Dodge Ridge in the Sierra Mountains. A friend of mine, who was a graduate from the City College of San Francisco Restaurant Program, owned the ski lodge that catered to youth groups. I would cook at the ski lodge and still have time to learn to ski. It was a great job that did not interfere with my college.

The owner and the Navy man were both very nice to me. I would make a small dinner and return to my room to work on my schoolwork. They would invite me to watch TV with them, but I wanted to get all my schoolwork completed by Friday so I could head for the mountains and the ski slopes.

One Friday night, after ski season ended, I went to bed and went to sleep. I would normally sleep with the sheet and covers over my head. Not sure why, but I have always slept that way. It was later that night when I heard a noise that woke me up.

When I took the covers off my head, the room was filled with smoke. My first thought was to break the window, climb out, and drop down to the ground as I was over the garage. Then I thought it might not be that bad so why not just go out the front door. I opened my bedroom door, and there was a lot more heat and very thick smoke in the hall. I ran down the hall and could see the fire in the living room and the flames.

I turned to my left and grabbed the doorknob. It was very hot, and it caused a small burn in the palm of my right hand. I did not have shoes on, and as I went down the stairs, there was broken glass on the landing and the stairs. I just ran over the glass in my bare feet. It was a miracle I did not cut my feet. I was only wearing my pj's because I did not take time to get dressed. I did not see anyone else in the home as I exited.

When I got down the stairs and went to the street, the fire department had just pulled up. One of the firemen asked me if there were any other people in the house. I looked around and could not see the other people from the house, so I told the fireman about the man and lady who also lived in the house. The fireman asked me to show him where I came out of the house. I went back up to the front door, and he opened the door. He looked in and said, "I am not going in there." Now the flames were up to the ceiling.

I moved to the other side of the street and watched the firemen put out the fire. By this time, a number of people had gathered to see what was going on. It was very cold in San Francisco that evening. The people were very nice, and one offered me their coat as I was not wearing much.

When the fire was out, the firemen told me the man was dead and must have fallen asleep on the sofa with a cigarette that started the fire. He had been drinking as he did on most nights.

The lady was found in the kitchen with the phone off the hook. She had tried to call the fire department but was overcome by the smoke and fell to the floor. She had also been drinking with the man. She was badly burned with third-degree burns over 50 percent of her body. The fireman said she would live three days and then die due to the burns. His prognosis was correct to the day.

The fireman let me return to my room to change my clothes and get what I needed. They were very concerned if I had a place to stay. A neighbor let me use their phone to call my friend in Sausalito, and I went there to stay for the remainder of the night.

The next morning was Saturday, and I returned to the house to get my personal things from my room. I remember thinking, "Is the man still on the sofa or has he been removed?" I was driving a red

VW but did not have that much to move: a small desk, clothes, and school books.

As I was leaving the house, I ran into the sister of the lady who owned the home. She was very upset about the fire and her sister. She got in my face and said, "How come you got out alive and they were dead and badly burned?" I did not have the heart to tell her they both had been drinking heavily. I felt that was someone else's job.

Later, I learned from the fire department it was a house some distance away that saw the flames and called the fire department. It must have been the fire trucks with the sirens that woke me, as I am a very sound sleeper.

On Monday, I returned to school and told a friend about the fire. I thought it was only by the grace of God that I was saved that night. **It was just not my time.** It makes one really reflect on their life.

I should have asked for Salvation. Now I know it was really a miracle that I survived unhurt that night. At that time in my life, I did not even know what Salvation was.

Why did God save my life? What plan did He have for me?

CHAPTER 22

The Blame Game

I was reading a list of court trials that ended in very unusual results. This is the story of just one of those trials.

A lady had purchased a new mobile home, such as a Winnebago. It was complete with a small bedroom and a small kitchen. She had a driver's license and decided to take a short trip in her new mobile home. While driving, she got hungry when she was on the freeway and decided to put on the cruise control and make some lunch in the kitchen. As most of us would guess, the mobile home went out of control, crashed, and was totaled.

At the trial, she stated there was nothing in the manual that stated she could not do just what she did. As a result, the jury ruled it was the manufacturer of the mobile home that was at fault and had to pay for the damages incurred by this person. This jury was certainly a jury of her peers. Today, people do not want to take responsibility for their actions.

It is said it takes a lifetime to develop a reputation that your word can be counted on, and it can be lost in a day. Are you a person of your word? Do you keep your word when you tell someone you will do something? Do you take responsibility when something goes wrong?

Today, people are more and more playing the "blame game." President Obama became very good at it. He blamed President Bush. He blamed Congress. He blamed security briefings. He blamed anyone he could.

More and more people do not want to take responsibility for their actions. It is an honest person who will say they made a mistake. It is an honest person who will take credit if they did something that did not work out as planned.

How America works: There is an excuse for everything!

Let's see if I understand how America works lately . . .

- If a woman burns her thighs on the hot coffee she was holding in her lap while driving, she blames the restaurant.
- If your teenage son kills himself, you blame the rock-and-roll music or musician he liked.
- If you smoke three packs of cigarettes a day for forty years and die of lung cancer, your family blames the tobacco company.
- If your daughter gets pregnant by the football captain, you blame the school for having a poor sex education program.
- If your neighbor crashes into a tree while driving home drunk, they blame the bartender.
- If your cousin gets AIDS because the needle he used to shoot up heroin was dirty, you blame the government for not providing clean ones.
- If your grandchildren are brats without manners, you blame television.
- If your friend is shot by a deranged madman, you blame the gun manufacturer.
- If a crazed person breaks into the cockpit, tries to kill the pilots at thirty-five thousand feet, and the passengers kill him instead, the mother of the deceased blames the airline.

I must have lived too long to understand the world as it is anymore. So if I die while I am sitting in front of my computer, I want to blame Bill Gates, OK?

Lesson: Take responsible actions, and take responsibility for your actions.

CHAPTER 23

America the Beautiful
One Nation under God

*"There is a way that appears to be right,
but in the end it leads to death"*
(Proverbs 14:12).

The United States of America was founded a short 241 years ago. It was founded on the principle that it would be **"one Nation under God."** We are a nation of laws, and many of those laws are based on the Bible. We have laws that one should not steal, kill, or give false witness. These are the most basic laws, and they should sound familiar as they are from God's Ten Commandments given to Moses.

It is rewarding to study how the Founding Fathers put together the new nation of America. It was a new experiment in government as all the nations at that time had kings or queens as the head of their country. America would be ruled by the people for the people. Much of the wording for the Constitution and Bill of Rights was taken from the Bible.

When Daniel Webster was writing his expanded dictionary, he used the Bible to define the words *man*, *woman*, and many others.

Many of the leaders at that time wanted the main book for schools to be the Holy Bible. That is how much the foundation of America was based on the Holy Bible and God's Word. Because so many people could not read, they decided the first schoolbook should be designed to teach children how to read. But make no mistake, God's Word was taught in the schools for many years.

For the first two hundred years, God has blessed our nation in so many ways because of our belief in God and His Word and because our leaders shared that strong belief in God. We have 5 percent of the world's population and 50 percent of the world's wealth. We have more freedom and more opportunity than any other country in the world. When we had to go to war such as World War I and II, we have not captured the nations concerned. We have not enslaved the people or extracted their wealth. Rather we have rebuilt those nations to be better than they were before the war. Japan is an example of one of the countries we helped after World War II. Germany was also rebuilt. This is in accordance with God's Word.

We have been the envy of the world. People living in other countries want to come to America for **freedom** and **opportunity** to make a better life. We have **not** done this alone but rather with **God's blessings**.

On September 11, 2001, there was an attack on the World Trade Center in New York City, the Pentagon in Washington, DC, and a United flight in Pennsylvania. Over three thousand Americans were killed by terrorists. One lady said, "**Where was God?**"

We have taken prayer to God out of our schools. We have taken the Pledge of Allegiance to our country and our flag with reference to "one Nation under God" out of our schools. We have taken the Ten Commandments and references to God out of our government buildings. We have tried to be so politically correct that we have forgotten we were founded as **"one Nation under God."**

(see Note 23-1)

In the heat of the American Civil War, one of President Lincoln's advisors said he was grateful God was on the side of the Union. Lincoln replied, "Sir, my concern is not whether God is on our side; my greatest concern is to be on God's side, for **God is always right**."

What a great challenge for us who assume God is there to support our plans, perspectives, decisions, and desires. However, Lincoln's reply reminds us even our best plans may not be near to what God desires (See Notes 23-2).

Remember, God will not always give us what we want, but He will always give us what we need.

Since the 1970s, America has moved further and further away from God's Word in the Holy Bible.

In 2014, a missionary from our church went to Central Africa to set up new churches and spread the word of Salvation through giving one's life to Jesus and receiving eternal life. The missionary asked the local minister if there were any schools in the area where he could share God's Word. The minister contacted local schools with five hundred elementary students from grades 1 to 6. The principal was a Christian and assembled five hundred students who all decided to give their lives to Jesus Christ and take Him as their personal Savior. We think we have freedom here in America, but this could not happen in America. **How free are we?**

The change in direction in the last fifty years has been disappointing. In the past, starting with the Founding Fathers, the emphasis has been on freedom of religion and that guiding philosophy that we are "**one Nation under God.**"

As we continue to refine the laws that guide our great nation, our laws, which I call "man's laws," have gotten further and further away from the laws of God as stated in the Holy Bible.

We cannot make everyone happy. America was founded as "**one Nation under God.**" Our great nation is 241 years old in 2017. In my seventy one years of living, I have seen America move away from God's Word and His teaching. Can we change the direction of our course and keep this country great? I don't think God will continue to bless America if we continue to make laws that are a contradiction to God's Word.

> *"Jesus looked at them and said, "With man this is impossible, but with God all things are possible"* (Matthew 19:26).

On June 26, 2015, the Supreme Court made their decision on the right of same-sex couples to marry. The court voted to grant same-sex marriage rights to all fifty states, and it's now the law of the land. The decision was split. The four conservative judges voted **NO**, and the five liberal judges voted YES. So in a five to four vote, it became law. **It is a dark day for America.**

Franklin Graham, the president of Samaritan's Purse and Billy Graham Evangelistic Association, in a Twitter post, said, **"The Supreme Court did not define marriage and therefore cannot redefine it."**

"Tolerance is the last virtue of a dying society," (Aristotle, 384–322 BC, a Greek philosopher, over three hundred years before the birth of Jesus Christ).

> *"But if you will not listen to me and carry out all these commands, and if you reject my decrees and abhor my laws and fail to carry out all my commands and so violate my covenant,*
> *then I will do this to you: I will bring on you sudden terror, wasting diseases and fever that will destroy your sight and sap your strength. You will plant seed in vain, because you enemies will eat it. I will set my face against you so that you will be defeated by your enemies; those who hate you and will rule over you, and you will flee even when no one is pursuing you. If after all this you will not listen to me, I will punish you for your sins seven times over"* (Leviticus 26:14–18).

Are we seeing God's judgment and punishment now?

I grew up in Southern California, and every few years, we would experience a forest fire, normally in the fall, after a really dry summer. Now we are seeing major forest fires every year in the entire southwestern states. Recently, I heard in the news there were fifteen major fires that were all out of control. Much of this was due to an extended four-to-five-year drought in California.

We have large storms in New Orleans and New Jersey that caused a lot of damage and loss of life.

We are also experiencing terrorism on a scale we have never seen before, starting with the four planes hijacked on September 11, 2001 and over three thousand Americans who lost their lives.

Right after the 9/11 terrorist attack, there were a lot of people who turned to their church for answers, but when it appeared that they were safe and had nothing to worry about, they left their churches. Now we see terrorism is very much alive in the United States.

Some people think of God as a spare tire you pull out when you have a problem with your life. You really should let God take control of the steering wheel of your life.

God's Word tells us we might receive judgment in the form of wasting diseases.

We are experiencing new diseases like AIDS and the Zika virus. Are these our judgment for turning away from God and His Word?

As we look at the changes in America we should be concerned with the daily changes and even more concerned with the changes from one decade to the next. It is ironic that we as a nation are headed in the direction to end up with the same type of country that our founding fathers left to establish a better nation in America.

The past will show us the right path to the future.

In the Old Testament of the Bible, there are many stories where the people were rewarded with God's blessings when they followed His Word and His Laws. There are also many stories where God's people worshipped other gods, and they were overrun by their enemies and taken slaves, such as the story of Babylon where the Israelites were enslaved for seventy years.

Our God is a good, caring, and loving God as He wants the best for all His children. He loves all His children, but He does not like sin and will not allow it to enter the kingdom of Heaven. When people sin, they are turning their backs on God and His Word in the Bible.

God is a jealous God and does not want us to follow other gods. As a nation, we have turned to other gods such as money, the stock market, sports, boats, cars, houses, clothing, and other material items.

The first of the Ten Commandments

"Thou shalt have no other Gods before me."

THE
TEN COMMANDMENTS

I. Thou shalt have no other Gods before me

II. Thou shalt not make unto thee
any graven image

III. Thou shalt not take the name
of the Lord thy God in vain

IV. Remember the sabbath day, to keep it holy

V. Honor thy father and thy mother

VI. Thou shalt not kill

VII. Thou shalt not commit adultery

VIII. Thou shalt not steal

IX. Thou shalt not bear false witness
against thy neighbor

X. Thou shalt not covet

Exodus 20

The lesson to be learned is we need God, and we need to change this nation back to our original values with God's blessing.

CHAPTER 24

God's Law and Man's Law

If God's Word in the Bible says it is wrong . . .
Then it is wrong!
Live to a higher standard.

We as a nation have moved away from God's law and moved to man's law, and we have lost our way! We have lost our moral compass of what is right and what is wrong. We have legalized sin in the name of the law.

The United States of America was founded on one major principle—that we would be "**one Nation under God.**" For almost two hundred years, this principle has not changed. However, during the last fifty years, we have seen a major shift in our government—mainly, the Supreme Court. The Supreme Court is doing a balancing act between our Founding Fathers statement that America would be "**one Nation under God**" and what our individual **freedoms are based on the Constitution**. Many times, the Supreme Court has weighed in on individual freedom rather than consider God's Word and God's law if we are going to continue to be defined as "**one Nation under God.**"

1.   **What does the Bible say about the institution of marriage?**

The Bible says the institution of marriage is a union of a man and a woman.

> *"But at the beginning of creation*
> *God 'made them male and female.'*
> *'For this reason a man will leave his father and*
> *mother and be united to his wife, and the two*
> *will become one flesh.' So they are no longer two,*
> *but one flesh. Therefore what God has joined*
> *together, let no one separate"* (Mark 10:6–9).

2.   **What does the Bible say about same-sex marriage?**

God's Word does not permit such marriages as they do not meet the definition of marriage as a union of a man and a woman as stated above.

Prior to June 26, 2015, thirty-six states had passed laws that allow same-sex marriages. This is against God's law. States were arguing that it is a "Constitutional" right to marry a person of the same gender.

If we are going to follow our heritage as a nation, we should first consider God's law when continuing to establish new laws or redefine our current laws.

The Supreme Court stated it is a Constitutional right for same-sex persons to marry in all fifty states, and the ruling stated that churches have the right to decide who they will marry and who they will not marry. I am sure this will also be tested by a future case in the Supreme Court.

The Supreme Court has once again legalized sin with this new ruling. This decision by the Supreme Court moved our society further away from God's Word and God's Laws.

3. **What does the Bible say about sexual relations between the same sex?**

Homosexuality exists in about 10 percent of the population. Many will say that is the way God made them. The Bible passage below indicates that in God's Word and God's law, being homosexual is a sin and it is "detestable."

This proves that being homosexual is a personal choice and not the way they were made by God. God's Word says homosexuality is a sin, and sin will not enter Heaven.

> *"4 You must obey my laws and be careful to follow my decrees. I am the LORD your God."*
> *22 Do not have sexual relations with a man as one does with a woman; that is detestable."*
> (Leviticus 18:4, 22)

4. **What does the Bible say about marriage of people who are nonbelievers?**

> *"Do not be yoked together with unbelievers"* (2 Corinthians 6:14).

Man's law does not address this requirement, but it might help the divorce rate to decrease, providing this was a law.

5. **What does the Bible say about divorce?**

Marriage is a covenant between God, a man, and a woman, and it should not be broken until death.

> *"Anyone who divorces his wife and marries another woman commits adultery, and the man who marries a divorced woman commits adultery"* (Luke 16:18).
>
> ——•——
>
> *"But I tell you that anyone who divorces his wife, except for sexual immorality, makes her the victim of adultery, and anyone who marries a divorced woman commits adultery"* (Matthew 5:32).

God has stated that a man and a woman should marry for life, till death do they part. Most all other circumstance, a divorce is considered adultery. Adultery is one of the Ten Commandments, and to commit adultery is a sin.

Man's law

Man's law does grant divorce with a limited waiting period that varies from state to state. Because of the ease of obtaining a divorce many couples enter marriage with the idea that if it does not work out, they will just get a divorce and go on with their lives.

6. What does the Bible say about sex outside of marriage?

> *"In order that the righteous requirement of the law might be fully met in us, who do not live in according to the flesh but according to the Spirit. Those who live according to the flesh have their minds set on what the flesh desires; but those who live in accordance with the Spirit have their minds set on what the Spirit desires. The mind governed by the flesh is death, but the mind governed by the Spirit is life and peace"* (Romans 8:4–6).

Man's law does permit sexual acts between two consenting adults over the age of eighteen. Due to the age of the birth control pill and abortions on demand, sexual activity outside of marriage has escalated. **We have lost our moral compass.**

7.   What do our laws say about prayer in schools?

In 1962, a law was established that removed prayer from our schools. One person challenged the practice of prayer in school based on the separation of church and state. Separation of church and state is often quoted to limit the use of God's word and prayer in schools, universities, and government buildings. The separation of church and state is not part of any law, as it was only stated in a letter by Thomas Jefferson. The point of his letter was to insure there was no state mandated religion. Religious Freedom was the main reason many of the pioneers moved to America. They were looking for the freedom to worship where they wanted.

Our founding fathers believed very strongly that schools should teach religion and moral values including the freedom to pray. Considering that the Bible was going to be the first textbook in American schools, one must see, we are heading in the wrong direction. The only reason the Bible was not the first text book in schools was because most of the people could not read. In 1690, *The New England Primer* was the first school textbook printed in America. Prior to that teachers used the Holy Bible imported from Europe. Even though the Bible was not the textbook, the wisdom of God's Word and the moral values of the Bible were taught in schools for over 325 years.

What has the effect been?

Our SAT scores have fallen. Sexually transmitted diseases have quadrupled. Teen pregnancies have skyrocketed, as has premarital sex and single-parent households. The divorce rate and violent crime have all shot through the roof. School and university shootings have increased. Haven't we learned yet what the effects will be when a nation removes prayer from its schools?

8. What does the Bible say about when life begins?

> *"The Spirit of God has made me;*
> *the breath of the Almighty gives me life."*
> (Job 33:4)
>
> ——•·•——
>
> *"Children are a heritage from the LORD,*
> *offspring a reward from him."*
> (Psalms 127:3)
>
> ——•·•——
>
> *"For you created my inmost being;*
> *you knit me together in my mother's womb.*
> *I praise you because I am fearfully*
> *and wonderfully made;*
> *your works are wonderful,*
> *I know that full well."*
> (Psalms 139:13–14)

In 1973, the landmark Supreme Court ruling of *Roe vs. Wade* gave women the right to abort their children. During the first forty years of that law, from January 1973 until January 2013, over fifty-five million babies have been killed due to abortion. That is 3,767 killings a day for 40 years!

This is man's law and not God's law.

Life is a gift from God, and the Bible says life starts at conception. Killing children by abortion is against God's law. It is not "Where has God been?" but rather "Where have we been?" and, more importantly, "Where are we headed?"

Man's law stated that a woman has a right over her body and she can abort a child any time before birth. This is in direct violation of God's Word as stated in the Ten Commandments: **"Thou shall not kill."**

There are two areas that are being argued.

a. **When does life start?** - Science can tell us with 3-D ultrasounds that we can definitely see there is life before birth. Currently, there is a petition to change the start of life from birth (man's definition) to starting at conception (God's law). Providing thirty-five states pass this petition, it will force the Supreme Court to reverse the *Roe vs. Wade* decision of 1973.

b. **A woman's rights over her body** - A woman does have every right over her body, until she has conceived a child. Then the child's right to life is greater than her right over her body or, more concisely, her right to have the child killed by abortion.

We are totally ignoring that children have a "right to life," and once conceived, that right is greater than a woman's right over her body.

People are just saying, "I don't care what God's law is. I just want what I want." If we are going to be "**one Nation under God**," we should change our current path and return to God.

America, with its current law from Roe vs. Wade**, as upheld by the Supreme Court, has allowed abortion to cause the death of ten times the six million deaths in the Holocaust of World War II. How can we call ourselves "one Nation under God"? As a country, we have lost our moral compass, and we have lost our way that once was God's way.**

God's law is clearly stated in the Ten Commandments: "Thou shall not kill."

When one is young, it is easy to make the wrong decision and sin. Providing you make your decisions ahead of time to follow God's Word and God's law, and really consider the long-range impact and consequences of your decisions, you will make better decisions.

> *"The acts of the flesh are obvious:*
> *sexual immorality, impurity and debauchery;*
> *idolatry and witchcraft; hatred, discord, jealousy,*
> *fits of rage, selfish ambition, dissensions,*
> *factions and envy; drunkenness, orgies and*
> *the like. I warn you, as I did before, that*
> *those who live like this will not inherit the*
> *kingdom of God"* (Galatians 5:19–21).

America was founded on God's Word in the Holy Bible, and in the beginning of our great country, most people lived by God's Word and God's law. I challenge you to live to a higher standard and live by God's Word. God loves you and wants the best for you and your life. That is why God's Word is a much higher standard than Man's law. Man's law cannot make sin legal when compared to God's Word. As one ages and matures, they realize how very important this is to one's success of finding true happiness.

It is never the wrong time
To do the right thing.
Live to a higher standard.

CHAPTER 25

What Has Happened to the USA?

What has happened to our way of life? America was founded on basic principles, but we have chosen a different path. What are the factors that have caused this to happen?

I think there are basically eleven factors:

1. We have taken God out of our schools.
2. The family unit has broken down.
3. Our country has moved from the right to the left.
4. Americas' reputation in the world has fallen.
5. Race relations are dividing the people.
6. Illegal Immigration and Drugs are out of control.
7. Government spending is out of control.
8. Our monetary system is in jeopardy of failing.
9. Our military is understaffed and under financed.
10. We are a country of laws, and that is being tested.
11. We are no longer "one Nation under God."

1. God taken out of our schools

I enjoy watching old Western movies. They display life as it was many years ago. The Bible was a central part of their lives, and farmers were God-fearing men focused on teaching their children the wisdom of the Bible. In the evening, the fathers would sit by the fireplace and read various Bible stories to his family.

At that time, farmers would not work on Sunday as the Ten Commandments state to keep the Sabbath holy for it is a day of rest. Some farmers were miles from the closest church. They would get their buggy or buckboard, attach a team of horses, and off they would go to church with the entire family. Church was a place of worship and a place for fellowship. Sometimes, a picnic was included as part of the fellowship, with games for the children.

Life was hard, and it was only as good as they could make it. There was no government assistance if the crops were not good. They relied on their neighbors for help in times of need. The Bible taught sharing and helping one's fellow man.

The children would learn good work habits from their parents. They would learn from the Bible stories and from watching their parents. They would see how their parents would interact with the fellow members of the church. It was a simpler time, but God's Word was the guiding light in their lives.

In addition to God's Word being taught at home, it was also taught in the schools.

Today, we have a dangerous society with killings in schools and universities, movie theaters, and many others places. We ask ourselves, "What went wrong with our young people that they take this path for their lives?" I believe the major contributing factor is the removal of God's Word from our school systems. Remember, for every action, there is a reaction.

A student enters a church and kills a number of the members of the church who were in a Bible study, and we ask why. Our government officials want to change the flag of South Carolina as it caused the hatred that pushed the student to kill. We are not doing a good job of connecting the dots to see the real reason that caused the problem. One of the reasons is God's Word and God's laws were taken out of our schools causing erosion of good moral values in our nation.

> *"All your children will be taught by the
> LORD, and great will be their peace"*
> (Isaiah 54:13).

2.   The family unit

Now in most of the homes that have two parents, both of them work. Life is more complicated and hectic. The time for church and fellowship is not a high priority for many families. People want bigger homes and newer cars; therefore, both parents work. Is it really worth the trade-off for spending time raising their children in a home with Christian values? Because of the hectic lifestyle, they say they are just too tired to go to church on Sunday.

There are more single-parent homes today. There are more teenage mothers who are not married. There is a lack of the guidance from a father figure in many families.

Today, children and teenagers have many distractions that they encounter. There is TV, radio, movies, cars, the internet, social media, cell phones, and video games to mention a few. These all offer some form of bad language, pornography, hate crime, racial bigotry, destruction, and killing. All these distract children from developing a strong moral platform for making good decisions. And they will just say, "There is no time for church."

Remember:

"We make time for what is important to us."
"Life is what we make it."

> *"What good is it for someone to gain the whole
> world, yet forfeit their soul?"* (Mark 8:36).

3. Conservative or liberal America?

Our country is currently in a phase to move to a more liberal form of government and education. This is happening at a relatively fast pace. When I was in high school, our country was experiencing a high rate of growth in the economy, and most people were feeling good about the peace in America after World War II. When I was in grade school, we said our allegiance to the "Stars and Strips" as "one Nation under God," and as part of school, we went to church on Wednesday afternoon.

People could get jobs and buy homes. It was a very good time in America. Since that time, our government has gotten larger, our national debt has increased, and our middle class is feeling a real difficulty to make ends meet even with both parents working. Many people think the solution is a larger government with more restrictions. Our best growth years were during the time President Regan was in office. His presidency made a number of changes that were good for business, the economy, jobs, and the middle class.

We have a very liberal Department of Education. It has a very liberal bias, and that is reflected in the selection of the lesson plans and direction of education from a national level. We have witnessed America fall from being one of the best educated countries to a country that does not offer competitive education with other countries. The decrease in test scores is not a result of a cut of funding, as we spend more money per student than any other country but our results fall short of excellence. We should return the management of our schools to the state level. The states would be competitive in striving for the best-educated students.

4. America's reputation in the world

During the last eight years, the reputation of America has decreased. We have made friends and deals with countries that say "death to America," and we have turned our backs on the countries that have been our allies during and since World War II.

President Obama manipulated a plan to make this happen. With one country, he stated, "If you use dangerous gases on your people, we will take action against you." He drew a line in the sand. But they crossed that line and gassed their people, resulting in many deaths, and he did nothing. This sent a message to other countries that he is a weak leader—that America is weak.

During this same eight years, we have seen terrorism increase in the world and in this country.

5. Race relations are dividing the people.

President Obama was elected in 2008, and race relations looked like they were going to get better. He made a great speech that America is not a collection of red and blue states but we are the United States of America. Since that time, we have seen a decrease of unity in America.

There are racial problems directed at the police across this nation with the "Black Lives Matter" group. Due to the economic policies of this administration, we have seen a large divide in the economic classes. The rich have gotten richer. We have more people on government welfare than ever in the history of the country. We have more people working in the government at 30 percent higher compensation than the general workforce for similar work. We have seen the middle class lose some of their earning power. We have the lowest percentage of our population working during the last fifty years. We need to get more of our people working and less on government welfare and smaller government.

6. Immigration is out of control.

Legal and illegal immigration is increasing. This has had a negative effect on the safety of America and our national debt. Many people visit America on visas and do not leave when their visas have expired. The government needs to be more accountable to find these people and send them to their home countries. We also need to stop the drugs that are entering America. They are having a very negative effect on our youth and causing an increase in crime. There are over 50,000 deaths each year in America due to drug abuse.

7.   Government spending is out of control.

Families in America have to live on a budget. This country is not living on a budget or even close to it. The president should provide leadership to bring our country together to solve big problems, but he just keeps on spending. Our national debt is twenty trillion dollars. There is a lot of waste in our government and a lack of accountability.

8.   Our monetary system is in jeopardy.

In 2008 the financial system in America saw the closing of many banks and businesses that caused a recession. The Federal Reserve decreased interest rates to almost one percent to help rebuild the financial system.

In addition, the Federal Reserve printed a lot of money to buy up questionable notes from banks to allow them to free up their financial system. The Federal Reserve called this QE1, QE2, and QE3. The QE stands for quantitative easing. This was printing money to try to fix the problem, but it did not solve the problem. It just kicked it down the road.

The year 2015 was the first year China has sold more US Treasury bonds than they bought. Where are they putting their money? They are buying gold.

In 2016, our economy is showing signs of decreasing growth even with the injection of low-priced capital with low-interest rates. We need continued growth to provide additional jobs for students entering the work force. At this time in history, many students are not finding employment when they graduate college and are having difficulty repaying their student loans. It is ironic these students that can't find jobs are the same young people that voted for the "Change" that President Obama was selling during his election campaign.

9. Our military is understaffed and underfinanced.

The main responsibility of the president and the federal government is the protection of America and its people.

The United States of America has the smallest number of military personnel and equipment since before World War II. To make things worse, the White House has been consistently interfering with military operations by putting many restrictions on the military brass in the way they are to do their jobs to keep America safe. We need to support our military leaders and give them the tools to win the war on terrorism.

Much of the military equipment needs to be updated. The military cannot get spare parts to keep the older planes and other equipment operational.

10. We are a country of laws, and it is being tested.

America was founded as a country of laws. There was a recent riot in Ferguson, Missouri. Many of the youths were rioting because an African-American young adult was shot. The rioting groups were taking to the streets in protest and were burning cars and businesses. Some of our elected personnel stated they have a right to protest. They do have a right to protest but not a right to damage the property of others to make a point. America is better than this.

We have two sets of standards. The rich and powerful politicians break the laws and are not prosecuted whereas the average citizen would be held accountable to the law.

11. We are no longer "one Nation under God."

Our Founding Fathers established the United States of America as a new nation. We were founded as "one Nation under God." Our money is printed with the words "In God we Trust," yet President Obama announced in a speech on August 3, 2014 that "America is no longer a Christian nation."

Leadership is so important. There is a saying about leadership, and it goes like this: **"The speed of the leader sets the speed of the pack."** This is true, whether it is a motorcycle gang, a Fortune 500 corporation, or a nation.

How can we return America to the years of prosperity for all?

> *"Jesus looked at them and said, 'With man this is impossible, but with God all things are possible'"* (Matthew 19:26).

The root of the problem

These eleven areas where America is experiencing very negative changes are related to one main cause. We have turned our backs on God and His wonderful Word providing wisdom in the Bible.

Only God knows the right path for our country to survive. If we are going to change our current direction in America, we need to turn to God and ask His help.

CHAPTER 26

Seventeen Inches

This is a story about a baseball coach and the wisdom he discovered while attending a coaches baseball convention. The wisdom he learned applies to coaching the game of baseball and also living the game of life. The author is unknown.

(Note 26-1)

In Nashville, Tennessee, during the first week of January 1996, more than four thousand baseball coaches descended upon the Opryland Hotel for the fifty-second annual American Baseball Coaches Association (ABCA) convention.

While I waited in line to register with the hotel staff, I heard other more veteran coaches rambling about the lineup of speakers scheduled to present during the weekend. One name, in particular, kept resurfacing, always with the same sentiment. "John Scolinos is here? Oh, man, worth every penny of my airfare."

"Who is John Scolinos?" I wondered. No matter, I was just happy to be there.

In 1996, Coach Scolinos was seventy-eight years old and five years retired from a college coaching career that began in 1948. He shuffled to the stage to an impressive standing ovation, wearing dark polyester pants, a light blue shirt, and a string around his neck, from which a home plate hung—a full-sized, stark-white home plate.

"Seriously," I wondered, "Who is this guy?"

After speaking for twenty-five minutes, not once mentioning the prop hanging around his neck, Coach Scolinos appeared to notice the snickering among some of the coaches. Even those who knew him had to wonder exactly where he was going with this or if he had simply forgotten about the home plate since he'd gotten on stage. Then, finally . . .

"You're probably all wondering why I'm wearing a home plate around my neck," he said, his voice growing irritable. I laughed along with the others, acknowledging the possibility. "I may be old, but I'm not crazy. The reason I stand before you today is to share with you, baseball people, what I've learned in my life and what I've learned about home plates in seventy-eight years."

Several hands went up when Scolinos asked how many Little League coaches were in the room. "Do you know how wide home plates are in Little League?" he asked.

After a pause, someone offered, "Seventeen inches?" It was more of a question than an answer.

"That's right," he said. "How about in Babe Ruth's day? Any Babe Ruth coaches in the house?"

Another long pause. "Seventeen inches?" came a guess from another reluctant coach.

"That's right," said Scolinos. "Now, how many high school coaches do we have in the room?"

Hundreds of hands shot up as the pattern began to appear.

"How wide are home plates in high school baseball?" he asked again.

"Seventeen inches," they said, sounding more confident.

"You're right!" Scolinos barked. "And you, college coaches, how wide are home plates in college?"

"Seventeen inches!" we said in unison.

"Any minor league coaches here? How wide are home plates in pro ball?"

"Seventeen inches!"

"RIGHT! And in the major leagues, how wide are home plates?"

"Seventeen inches!"

"SE-VEN-TEEN INCHES!" he confirmed, his voice bellowing off the walls. "And what do they do with a big-league pitcher who can't throw the ball over seventeen inches?"

Pause.

"They send him to Pocatello!" he hollered, drawing raucous laughter. "What they don't do is this. They don't say, 'Ah, that's OK, Jimmy. You can't hit a seventeen-inch target? We'll make it eighteen inches or nineteen inches. We'll make it twenty inches so you have a better chance of hitting it. If you can't hit that, let us know so we can make it wider still. Say, twenty-five inches.'"

Then he continued. "Coaches!" Pause. "What do we do when our best player shows up late to practice? When our team rules forbid facial hair and a guy shows up unshaven? What if he gets caught drinking? Do we hold him accountable, or do we change the rules to fit him? Do we widen the home plate?"

The chuckles gradually faded as four thousand coaches grew quiet, the fog lifting as the old coach's message began to unfold. He turned the plate toward himself and, using a Sharpie, began to draw something. When he turned it toward the crowd, pointed up, a house was revealed, complete with a freshly drawn door and two windows.

"This is the problem in our homes today, with our marriages, with the way we parent our kids, and with our discipline. We don't teach accountability to our kids, and there is no consequence for failing to meet the standards. We widen the plate!" he said.

There was another pause. Then, to the point at the top of the house, he added a small American flag.

"This is the problem in our schools today. The quality of our education is going downhill fast, and teachers have been stripped of the tools they need to be successful and to educate and discipline our young people. We are allowing others to widen the home plate! Where is that getting us?" he asked.

There was silence in the room.

He replaced the flag with a cross then he continued. "And this is the problem in the church, where powerful people in positions of authority have taken advantage of young children, only to have such a crime swept under the rug for years. Our church leaders are widening the home plate for themselves! And we allow it.

"And the same is true with our government. Our so-called representatives make rules for us that don't apply to them. They take bribes from lobbyists and foreign countries. They no longer serve us. We allow them to widen the home plate, and we see our country falling into a dark abyss while we watch."

I was amazed. At a baseball convention, where I expected to learn something about curveballs and bunting and how to run better practices, I had learned something far more valuable. From an old man with a home plate strung around his neck, I had learned something about life, myself, my own weaknesses, and my responsibilities as a leader. I had to hold myself and others accountable to that which I know to be right, lest our families, our faith, and our society continue down an undesirable path.

"If I am lucky," Coach Scolinos concluded, "You will remember one thing from this old coach today. It is this. If we fail to hold ourselves to a higher standard—a standard of what we know to be right, if we fail to hold our spouses and our children to the same standards, if we are unwilling or unable to provide a consequence when they do not meet the standard, and if our schools and churches and our government fail to hold themselves accountable to those they serve, there is but one thing to look forward to." With that, he held the home plate in front of his chest, turned it around, and revealed its dark black backside. "Dark days are ahead."

Coach Scolinos died in 2009 at the age of ninety-one, but not before touching the lives of hundreds of players and coaches, including mine. Meeting him at my first ABCA convention kept me returning year after year, looking for similar wisdom and inspiration from other coaches. He is the best clinic speaker the ABCA has ever known because he was so much more than a baseball coach.

This convention was in the year 1996, and that is twenty years ago. Looking at America today, it seems we have just widened the home plate over the last twenty years and we continue down the same path. It is only with God's help that we can turn our direction around and live by higher standards. (Note 26-2)

"Jesus looked at them and said, 'With man this is impossible, but with God all things are possible'" (Matthew 19:26).

CHAPTER 27

Paradox of Our Time

Paradox: something to really think about
Do you like where we are headed?

As delivered via e-mail. This was written before 2001, as we were not at war at that time in history. However, this is still true today.

This is so true, it is scary. This was written by Dr. Bob Moorehead, a pastor in Washington State.

> "The paradox of our time in history is that we have taller buildings, but shorter tempers; wider freeways, but narrower viewpoints.
>
> We spend more, but have less. We buy more, but enjoy it less.
>
> We have bigger houses and smaller families; more conveniences, but less time.
>
> We have more degrees, but less sense; more knowledge, but less judgment; more experts, yet more problems; more medicine, but less wellness.

We have multiplied our possessions, but reduced our values. We talk too much, love too seldom, and hate too often.

We've learned how to make a living, but not a life. We've added years to life, not life to our years.

We've been all the way to the moon and back, but have trouble crossing the street to meet a new neighbor. We've conquered outer space, but not inner space.

We've cleaned up the air, but polluted the soul. We've split the atom, but not our prejudice.

We have higher incomes, but lower morals. We've become long on quantity, but short on quality.

These are the times of big men and small character; steep profits and shallow relationships.

These are the times of world peace, but domestic warfare; more leisure, but less fun; more kinds of food, but less nutrition.

These are days of two incomes, but more divorce; fancier houses, but broken homes.

It is a time when there is much in the showroom window and nothing in the stockroom.

A time when technology can bring this letter to you, and a time when you can choose either to share this insight, or just hit delete . . ."

CHAPTER 28

The Seven Wonders of the World

A teacher was asking her class to list the Seven Wonders of the World. As each student in the class started to make a list, one girl was perplexed by the question. Then she started to make her list.

Most of the students listed places like the Great Wall of China, the Roman Coliseum in Italy, and the Taj Mahal in India.

The one young girl was still having problems with her list. The teacher asked if she was having a problem, and she said there were so many she could not list just seven. The teacher said, "Let me see your list, and maybe I can help you."

This was her list:

1. The wonder of sight.
2. The wonder of hearing
3. The wonder of taste.
4. The wonder of speech.
5. The wonder of touch.
6. The wonder of smell.
7. The wonder of the brain
8. The wonder of love
9. The wonder of God
10. The wonder of friendship

11. The wonder of Salvation
12. The wonder of eternal life.
13. The wonder of creation.

When we get older, we sometimes lose one or more of these wonders, and when we miss them, we really do see how wonderful they are. We don't really appreciate them until they are lost.

We have so much that we can learn from our children.

CHAPTER 29

Recall Notice

This recall notice is a humorous but honest look at our country, society, and the entire world. There is a lot of truth in this humor and the statement that is being made.

Worldwide Manufacturers' Recall

The maker of all human beings (GOD) is recalling all units manufactured, regardless of make or year, due to a serious defect in the primary and central component of the heart.

This is due to a malfunction in the original prototype units, code name Adam and Eve, resulting in the reproduction of the same defect in all subsequent units. This defect has been identified as "Subsequential Internal Nonmorality," more commonly known as SIN, as it is primarily expressed.

Some of the symptoms include the following:

1. Loss of direction
2. Foul vocal emissions
3. Amnesia of origin

4. Lack of peace and joy
5. Selfish or violent behavior
6. Fearfulness
7. Idolatry
8. Rebellion

The manufacturer, who is neither liable nor at fault for this defect, is providing factory-authorized repair and service free of charge to correct this defect.

The Repair Technician, **JESUS**, has most generously offered to bear the entire burden of the staggering cost to these repairs.

The number to call for repair in all areas is: P-R-A-Y-E-R.

Once connected, please upload your burden of **SIN** through the **REPENTANCE** procedure. Next, download **ATONEMENT** from the Repair Technician, **JESUS**, into the heart component.

No matter how big or small the SIN defect is, **JESUS** will replace it with the following:

1. Love
2. Joy
3. Peace
4. Patience
5. Kindness
6. Faithfulness
7. Gentleness
8. Self-control

Please see the operating manual, the BIBLE (Best Instructions Before Leaving Earth), for further details on the use of these fixes.

WARNING: Continuing to operate the human being unit without correction voids any manufacturer warranties, exposing the unit to the dangers and problems too numerous to list, and will result in the human unit being permanently impounded. For free emergency service, call on **JESUS**.

DANGER: The human being units not responding to this recall action will have to be scrapped in the furnace. The SIN defect will not be permitted to enter Heaven so as to prevent contamination of the facility. Thank you for your attention!

—GOD

P.S. Please assist where possible by notifying others of this important recall notice. You may contact the Father any time by "Knee Mail."

Because HE lives!

Working for **GOD** has many benefits, and **His** retirement plan is **out of this world!**

CHAPTER 30

Chicken in a Blizzard
One Person Can Make a Difference

GOD does work in mysterious ways.

Note 30-1

In 2013, Chick-fil-A made national headlines when company president Dan Cathy spoke out in support of traditional marriage. Liberals and gays became unglued and launched massive protests against the restaurant chain. Several mayors spoke out saying they would not allow any more Chick-fil-A's to be built in their cities.

They tried boycotting the Christian-owned company, but that backfired. Instead, Chick-fil-A had a world record day with many locations selling out of food to hundreds of thousands of supporters. Is it any surprise that the only news the liberal mainstream media has reported concerning Chick-fil-A has been the negative?

During the winter of 2015, an ice storm hit the south. The mainstream media showed footage of miles of cars stranded on the frozen interstates. Several national news broadcasts that I saw reported about school kids trapped on busses for almost twenty-four hours because of all of the ice and parents going frantic wondering where their kids were.

In all of the icy gloom and doom, I bet you didn't hear about the heroic and generous actions of a Chick-fil-A along Highway 280 in Birmingham, Alabama, did you?

Mark Meadows, owner of the Chick-fil-A, closed early the day of the storm and sent all of his employees home. However, the employees and Meadows soon discovered they were not going to be able to get home with all of the stranded motorists stuck on the roads. Some of the cars near the restaurant had been stranded for up to seven hours.

Meadows and his employees fired up the kitchen and began preparing chicken sandwiches as fast as they could. They prepared several hundred sandwiches, and then Meadows and his staff headed out and began distributing the hot meals to the stranded motorists on both sides of Highway 280.

Some of the drivers tried to pay them for the sandwiches, but Meadows and his employees refused to take a single penny. Audrey Pitt, manager of the Chick-fil-A, explained why. "This company is based on taking care of people and loving people before you're worried about money or profit. We were just trying to follow the model that we've all worked under for so long and the model that we've come to love. There was really nothing else we could have done but try to help people any way we could."

However, Meadows and Pitt were not through with their Good Samaritan efforts. They helped push cars off the roads and up inclines and whatever else they could do to help. Then they kept the restaurant open overnight so stranded motorists could have a warm place to be. A number of motorists slept in booths or on the benches.

Then in the morning, they again fired up the kitchen and prepared chicken biscuits for their overnight guests, and once again, they refused to accept any payment. During that twenty-four-hour period, this Chick-fil-A restaurant opened their kitchen, doors, and hearts to hundreds of stranded motorists, and they did so refusing to accept any payment. As one source put it, Meadows and his staff lived up to the words Jesus spoke in Matthew 25:35: *"For I was hungry and you gave me something to eat, I was thirsty and you gave me something to drink, I was a stranger and you invited me in."*

Their actions were truly generous and heroic as they also braved the frigid temperatures to hand out hundreds of hot meals to complete strangers. I bet you never heard anything about this from the mainstream media. Their liberal bias and intolerance would never allow them to report on a Christian company doing something so positive for so many. (Note 30-2)

I spent my entire career in the restaurant business, and most businesses are more concerned with cutting labor cost and increasing profits. Chick-fil-A has a different operating philosophy that is grounded in God's Word in the Bible. They are more concerned with the customer, the service level, and the quality of the product than just profits and giving in to what most people think is socially acceptable. God has blessed this company for their operating philosophy to live by God's Word.

We need to support this and other Christian companies that are trying to spread the good news of the gospel through their daily work.

A side note: Samuel Truett Cathy, the founder of Chick-fil-A and father of the current president and CEO, passed away on September 8, 2014.

Chick-fil-A is the only food service company where every location is closed on Sunday in recognition of the Sabbath—a day of rest, as stated by God's Word in the Bible, and one of the Ten Commandments. Because of the founder's strong Christian beliefs, this company has been blessed by God with tremendous success. **It is a shining example of God's work in America.**

God's Word is the philosophy that guides Chick-fil-A, and God has blessed the company.

CHAPTER 31

Working in the Vineyard

This story is called a Parable, that is an earthly story with a heavenly meaning. This Bible story I really love as it teaches me the glory and grace of the Lord. This is a paraphrase of the story in the Holy Bible, The Parable of the Workers in the Vineyard (Matthew 20, 1–16)

The story starts by saying that the Kingdom of Heaven is like a landowner who went out early in the morning to hire workers for his vineyard. He agreed to pay the workers one denarius for a day's work. A denarius was the usual daily wage for a day laborer. Some started early in the morning, and some started at nine and some at noon. Some started at three in the afternoon, and some did not start until five. But they all got the same amount of pay—one denarius for their work. Some said that was not fair. The people who worked longer should be paid more. The owner said he does this because he is generous.

The story is not about working in the vineyard but rather when a person decides to take the wonderful gift of Salvation as offered by our Lord. The people who take Salvation early in their life or late in their life get the same wonderful gift of Salvation, including eternal life in the Heavenly Kingdom of God. Wow, what a blessing!

If you take Jesus to be your personal Lord and Savior early in life, you get the same wonderful blessing of eternal life in Heaven and you get to live with the grace and guidance of God your entire life. I took Jesus as my personal Savior late in life and will receive the same beautiful gift of eternal life in Heaven. I do wish I had taken the Lord's gift earlier as there is so much beauty and wisdom in God's Word in the Bible and allowing God to direct our life.

There were so many times when a voice told me I was not good enough to do something or I was not smart enough. Now I know it was Satan, and when I hear that negative voice, I just don't listen to it.

Looking back, if I had God in my life, I would have made so many choices differently.

Remember, it is the lessons we learn from the past that show us the right path to the future. Learn from my mistakes as I know now there is a better way.

> *"For the grace of God has appeared that offers Salvation to all people. It teaches us to say 'No' to ungodliness and worldly passions, and to live self-controlled, upright and godly lives in this present age, while we wait for the blessed hope—the appearing of the glory of our great God and Savior, Jesus Christ, who gave himself for us to redeem us from all wickedness and to purify for himself a people that are his very own, eager to do what is good. These, then, are the things you should teach. Encourage the rebuke with all authority. Do not let anyone despise you"* (Titus 2:11–15).

Religion is when man reaches up to God. Salvation is when God reaches down to man.

CHAPTER 32

Wisdom and Knowledge
for Your Future

Knowledge is facts, information, and skills acquired by a person through experience or education. It is the theoretical or practical understanding of a subject.

Wisdom is the experience, knowledge, and good judgment. It is the quality of being wise in the application of knowledge.

If you know about electricity that is knowledge.

If you know not touch the inside of a light socket, that is wisdom.

True wisdom - Take God's truth from the Bible, and apply it to your life.

> *"Blessed are those who find wisdom,*
> *those who gain understanding,*
> *for she is more profitable than silver*
> *and yields better returns than gold.*
> *She is more precious than rubies;*
> *nothing you desire can compare with her."*
> (Proverbs 3:13–15)

> *"But the wisdom that comes from heaven is first of all pure; then peace-loving, considerate, submissive, full of mercy and good fruit, impartial and sincere"* (James 3:17).

This book only touches on some of the wonderful information, stories, knowledge, history, and wisdom of God's Word in the Holy Bible.

As I worked, putting this book together to help teens and young adults, I have enjoyed my research of the Bible and have learned so much. Sometimes, when we try to help others, we end up learning and helping ourselves. **A man never stands as tall as when he stoops to help a child.**

Hopefully, some of the wisdom in these pages will help you and other teens and young adults really think about their choices, decisions, the possible consequences and allow God to direct your lives.

Education can never be taken from you.

When I graduated from Cornell University in June of 1969, I had learned a lot of great information—business knowledge, business systems, financial analysis, personal investing, restaurant design, and computers. As I look back at my life, I did not really apply what I had learned. Now the following statement rings true to my ears. This is so simple yet so true.

The key to your success in life will be in wisely applying everything you have learned.

CHAPTER 33

"To Infinity and Beyond"
My Challenge to You

Buzz Lightyear made this saying popular in the *Toy Story* movie. Can one really go beyond infinity? By definition infinity is "unbounded space, time, or quantity." I know this saying was a play on the meaning of each word. It is like an oxymoron where the definition of one word is the direct opposite of the other word. Such as jumbo shrimp. It is like saying big small. How can something be big and small at the same time? If space or something else goes on forever, can one go beyond that distance?

Another term that is difficult to get one's mind around is eternal life. By definition, *eternal* means "lasting or existing forever, without end or beginning." Jesus offers eternal life in the kingdom of God to those who ask to be forgiven for past sins, state they will try to live a sin-free life, and surrender their lives to Jesus for the life He has for them.

In a recent Sunday night sermon, the Associate Pastor of Children and Families, Tom Toombs, told the following story.

If you were to take a white rope and start at the pulpit of the church, run the rope to the back of the sanctuary, return the rope up to the pulpit of the church, then return to the back of the sanctuary again and continue until the church floor is totally covered with the white rope. Next, you would go outside of the church, and the rope would cover the entire city of Maryville, Tennessee. Next, the rope would cover the entire city of Knoxville, Tennessee, then cover the entire state of Tennessee. Next, it would continue to cover all of the other states in the United States. Then the rope would go over the Atlantic Ocean and cover Europe. Then the rope would cover Russia, Asia, and Africa.

This would be a very long rope, and it would go on forever. The first inch of the rope is painted red, and the rest of the rope is white. This rope represents your life, and the one inch that is red represents the time you are on Earth. If you are on Earth for such a short amount of time compared to the rest of your life, would it not be smart to use your time on Earth to prepare for your afterlife?

Where are YOU going to spend ETERNITY?

That is the question you need to ask yourself. Be honest with yourself. This will be the most important decision you will need to make in your life on earth.

Once you ask Jesus for the beautiful gift of Salvation, you start to see the benefits. You will not feel alone as God will be with you.

Once I received Salvation and saw the change in myself, my only regret was I didn't have the faith to ask Jesus for Salvation much earlier in my life.

You can be confident that God knows all the answers and wants the best for you and your life. Do not worry about daily problems. Just follow God's direction. You will find you have more confidence because if you follow God's direction, you will receive the benefits of God's plan for your life. That is my challenge to you. You could do nothing, or you could ask for the wonderful gift of Salvation, given by the grace of God.

CHAPTER 34

In Closing

"**What we do for ourselves dies with us. What we do for others and the world remains and is immortal**" (Albert Pike, an English author who died in 1851, note 34-1). This is still true and very relevant today.

"**History happens when a man meets a man, and miracles happen when a man meets God!**" (Billy Kim, note 34-2).

Take the wisdom in this book and learn from my mistakes. God loves you and wants the best for you.

What makes a person great in the eyes of the world?

In the United States of America, we have been fortunate to have a number of really great leaders. When times are difficult, leaders show us the way to a better life, and they have achieved greatness.

Ronald Reagan was a great president, and he turned the nation around and put it on the right path for growth and prosperity.

President Lincoln made the difficult decision to keep the nation together at a crucial time in our history, and he achieved greatness.

Greatness is achieved by the number of lives one's life affects. The greatest person of all time is Jesus Christ as He has had and will continue to have a profound impact on so many people's lives. He is also great because He is the Son of God.

God has a plan for your life. We might not always understand His plan, but have faith and follow His plan and you will be blessed.

The Miracle of 2016

Much of News in 2016 was about the Presidential race between Hilary Clinton and Donald Trump. Clinton was offering a continuation of President Obama's administration and agenda. Trump was offering change, "To make America Great Again."

Both candidates worked very hard to sell their vision of America to all Americans. The News media is very liberal and thus was pushing Clinton, the liberal candidate and down playing her issue of questionable honesty and integrity. The news media was also running many stories that were not favorable to Trump as he was the conservative candidate. Both candidates were considered "far less than perfect" by the majority of voters.

When the polls started to evaluate the voters' wishes Clinton seemed less disliked than Trump and was ahead in the polls. Week after week the polls indicated that Clinton was predicted to win by as much as 75% to 95% certainty. She also had the strongest ground game to get out the voters.

On November 8, 2016 Donald Trump won the Presidency and also won a majority in the House of Representatives and the Senate.

How could so many people have it so wrong?

The media was wrong

The polls were wrong

This is why I call it the Miracle of 2016

> *Jesus looked at them and said,*
> *"'With man this is impossible, but with God*
> *all things are possible'"*
> (Matthew 19:26).

It is my personal Hope that this will be a return to stronger conservative values in our Government and return to God's Word and God's ways. But people can't do this alone. We need to ask God's Blessing and God's Help.

CHAPTER 35

God's Plan for My Life

Throughout the stories of my life, I have been consistent in saying "I have been fortunate" or that "God has blessed my life." I know now that the situations where I have experienced a positive ending were a result of God's work. How do I know? Because the Bible tells me so.

> *"Don't be deceived, my dear brothers and sisters. Every good and perfect gift is from above, coming down from the Father of the heavenly lights, who does not change like shifting shadows"* (James 1:16–17).

Sometimes, I think this might have been God's plan for my life—to share the wisdom from my life to help teens and young adults with the difficult choices they will make in their lives and help them find the glory and grace of the Lord.

Let God bless your life.
Just ask Him.
You have so much to gain.

Therefore, I urge you, brothers and sisters, in view of God's mercy, to offer your bodies as a living sacrifices, holy and pleasing God - this is your true and proper worship. Do not conform to the pattern of this world, but be transformed by the renewing of your mind. Then you will be able to test and approve what God's will is - his good, pleasing and perfect will. (Romans 12:1-2)

The End
There is no end to the love, mercy, and grace of God.

RECOMMENDED READING LIST

Once I received the gift of Salvation from Jesus I wanted to know more. Below are just of few of the books, letters and daily scripture that have helped my understanding of God's Word and God's Plan for every life He has ever created.

The Holy Bible, NIV God has blessed my entire life, even before I received the gift of Salvation from Our Lord Jesus on June 30, 2013. I enjoy reading the Holy Bible and leading more about the history, stories, parables, knowledge and wisdom contained in the many books of the Bible.

Our Daily Bread Ministry Starting each day with the story and Bible scripture has provided knowledge and wisdom to see each day in a new light. Free for the asking.

"A Letter from Larry" by Larry Perry This is a free publication that is sent via e-mail. These are inspirational Christian stories that deal with a number of subjects. The story of "seventeen inches" in this book was used with permission from Larry Perry and is an example of the type of stories in his letters. I highly recommend "A Letter from Larry".

"The Purpose Driven Life" by Rick Warren This book provides a clear and organized picture of God's plan for all his children, for now and for eternity. This book contains over 1,200 Bible Scriptures and is a must read for everyone.

NOTES

Note: All scripture for this book was taken from the New International Version (NIV) of the Holy Bible. Except when using the quotations from Our Daily Bread.

Chapter 1: Note 1-1
Statistics from researching family life in America
By the Southern Baptist Council

Chapter 3: Note 3-1 thru Note 3-2
Taken from Our Daily Bread, Book dated November 16, 2014
Copyright 2016 by Our Daily Bread Ministries, Grand Rapids, MI.
Used by permission. All rights reserved.

Chapter 4 Note 4-1
"My Way"
Written by Paul Anka

Chapter 12: Note 12-1 thru Note 12-2
Taken from Our Daily Bread, at the end of Book dated September, October, and November 2014
Copyright 2016 by Our Daily Bread Ministries, Grand Rapids, MI.
Used by permission. All rights reserved

Chapter 13: Note 13-1
LifeWay: http://www.lifeway.com/

Chapter 15: Note 15-1
Story from the internet. Professor's name and author's name not available via the internet.

Chapter 18: Notes 18-1 thru Note 18-2
Taken from Our Daily Bread, Book dated May 13, 2015
Copyright 2016 by Our Daily Bread Ministries, Grand Rapids, MI.
Used by permission. All rights reserved

Chapter 23: Notes 23-1 thru 23-2
Taken from Our Daily Bread, Book dated December 3, 2014
Copyright 2016 by Our Daily Bread Ministries, Grand Rapids, MI.
Used by permission. All rights reserved

Chapter 26: Note 26-1thru 26-2
"Seventeen Inches"
Provided by Larry Perry- with permission for use.
Author Unknown

Chapter 30: Note 30-1 thru 30-2
Story of "Chicken in a Blizzard"
From SFAW.org website. (Scriptures For America Worldwide)
Author Unknown.

Chapter 34 Note 34-1
Albert Pike, an English author that died in 1851.

Chapter 34 Note 34-2
From the book The Life of Billy Kim: From Houseboy to World Evangelist

ABOUT THE AUTHOR

David M. Hoof

David grew up in Southern California in the town of Glendale, where he learned to sail, scuba dive, and snow ski.

He earned an Associate Degree from the Hotel and Restaurant Department at the City College of San Francisco and a Bachelor of Science Degree in Hotel Administration from Cornell University.

He has gained wisdom from the many choices and decisions he has made during his life and the consequences of his decisions. He has learned there is a better way—a much better way!

At the age of sixty-eight, David found the Lord and was born again. His spiritual life was born, and he discovered what was missing in his life.

It is David's goal to share his wisdom with teens and young adults so they can make better decisions in their lives and avoid some of the errors that he made.

It is the choices we make that direct the path of our life.

David and his wife Susan live in Maryville, Tennessee. They enjoy time spent with their children and grandchildren.

You can't take your material possessions or wealth to Heaven, but you can take your children.

May God bless you.

CPSIA information can be obtained
at www.ICGtesting.com
Printed in the USA
LVHW08s0000280718
585097LV00001BA/10/P

9 781641 400060